To Keith →
Cook well, Eat well, Live
Pura Vida, Chef Dave

Cooking at LA CUSINGA with CHEF OF THE JUNGLE

DAVID L. MAHLER

#273

Copyright 2012 © David L. Mahler

First edition
Notice of Rights: All rights reserved. No part of this book may be reproduced in any form or by any electronic or mechanical means including information storage and retrieval systems without permission in writing from the author, except by a reviewer.

ISBN No. 978-0-615-66579-5

TABLE of CONTENTS

- PHILOSOPHY/WHO WE WERE/WHAT WE DID 5
- WHAT MADE LA CUSINGA SPECIAL 6
- RECIPES 7
  - SOUPS 9
    - Roasted Tomato 9
    - Curried Cauliflower 10
    - Carrot/Beet/Ginger 11
    - Spinach/Scallion 12
    - Roasted Summer Vegetable 13
  - SALADS 14
    - Basic Dressing 14
    - Dressing Variations 15
  - SALAD ADDITIONS 16
    - Marinated/Pickled Beets 16
    - Roasted Red Peppers 16
    - Roasted Garlic 17
    - Palmito (Hearts of Palm) 19
    - Frijoles Tiernos 21
    - Marinated Cucumbers 23
    - Cherry Tomatoes/Tomato Marinade 23
  - CROSTINI 24
    - Goat Cheese/Roasted Garlic/Green Herb Spread 24
    - Jungle Pesto 25
  - FISH COOKING 25
    - Grilling Fish 27
    - Roasting Fish 29
    - Cooking Tuna 29
  - SALSAS/SAUCES 30
    - Mango Salsa 30
    - Pineapple-Ginger Salsa 31
    - Papaya-Mandarina "Citrus-ette" 31
    - Thai Style Coco-Ginger Sauce 32
    - Green Gazpacho Salsa 33
    - Roasted Tomato/Caper Sauce 33
    - Green Herb Aioli 34
    - Salsa De La Jungla 35
  - SHRIMP 36
    - Jungle Shrimp "Chef Dave" 37
    - Yucatán Style Shrimp 37
  - CHICKEN COOKING 39
    - Cooking Chicken Breasts 39
    - Cooking Chicken Legs 41
    - Braised Chicken Legs 41
  - VEGETABLE COOKING 42

TABLE of CONTENTS cont.

- Green Bean and Broccoli Sauté 43
- Chinese Long Bean Sauté 43
- Braised Greens 44
- Choy 44
- Ayote 45
- Roasted Ayote 45
- Roasted Stuffed Ayote 47
- Ratatouille "Cusinga Style" 49
- STARCH SIDES 50
  - Rices/Arroz 50
  - Achiote Rice 50
  - Yucatán Style Green Rice 51
  - Jambalaya Rice 52
  - Gingered Risotto 53
- POTATOES 54
  - Green Herb Mashed Potatoes 54
  - Camote-Plantain Purée 55
  - Frijoles Tiernos (Hot) 55
- DESSERTS 57
  - Flourless (Almost) Chocolate Cake 58
  - Mandarina Pound Cake 60
  - "Not Your Mother's" Pineapple Upside Down Cake 61
  - Basque-Style Almond Torte 64
  - Caramelized Banana Tart 66
- ICE CREAM 67
  - Vanilla Bean Ice Cream 67
  - Mountain Blackberry Ice Cream 68
  - Organic Cacao Ice Cream 69
  - Caramelized Banana Ice Cream 70

GLOSSARY OF TERMS/EXPLANATIONS 71
COOKING TERMS 74
A FEW NOTES AND THOUGHTS ON COOKING 76
CREDITS 76
INDEX 78

PHILOSOPHY/WHO WE ARE/WHAT WE DID

I returned to La Cusinga in January 2009 with a dream in mind. I wanted to create a cuisine that would bridge the gap between what La Cusinga offered their guests physically and spiritually, and what their guests were putting in their bodies when they ate here.

Just as La Cusinga represents a sustainable form of eco-tourism, there was no reason that we could not offer a cuisine that reflected that same sustainability. The mission was to show not just our guests but also the people of this community that it was possible to create delicious, serious, mostly organic food using entirely local ingredients.

It was a vision that would support local farmers, fishermen, and food artisans and one that would create a new cuisine of coastal Costa Rica. I visit the markets each week to talk with growers and to develop the relationships that will be mutually beneficial as Costa Rica experiences its rapid growth on an international level. Dairy farmers, cheesemakers, rice farmers, ceramic artists, vanilla growers, and cacao farmers—all are included in this vision.

I am often asked if I cook entirely locally and my answer, somewhat surprised, is always, "Yes, of course, why wouldn't I?" This should be every chef's dream, to be able to provide the food for his or her guests with ingredients grown less than an hour away. Between the produce we grow here at the Lodge, the lovely organics we buy from our loyal and local farmers, and the fish that come from the ocean we can see from our kitchen, we have created a cuisine here at La Cusinga that is original and unique to this area.

What we are doing is by no means unique internationally; after all, the French have been using this model for years and the United States is home to a huge "farm to table" sensibility. But here in Costa Rica our world class fish and produce have been pushed to the side in an effort to create a more homogenous cuisine for tourists. I don't believe we have to do that and I believe that the ingredients we get here at tiny La Cusinga rival those of any kitchen in the world.

I am proud of the food we serve at La Cusinga. I am proud that organic growers here have risen to the challenge of producing top flight produce and I am proud to be able to go right to the boats where our fish are caught. But mostly I am proud to be able to put food on our tables here that honors and respects the hard work of John and Bella, of Geinier and Henry, and of all the people who make La Cusinga the world class eco-lodge that it is.

Chef Dave

WHAT MADE LA CUSINGA SPECIAL

When I was writing this book I asked John Tresemer, the owner and visionary behind La Cusinga, if he would be kind enough to write a few words for me describing his vision and his feelings for what he had created. John and his wife Bella took ownership of La Cusinga in 1973 and have slowly, patiently and respectfully developed the property into what it is today.

"I sensed the natural magic of La Cusinga when I first came as a college student and I still feel it decades later. One of my greatest satisfactions occurs when a visitor also senses that magic and communicates that feeling to me.

"What makes La Cusinga special is what we didn't do with it. We didn't develop and expand like real estate and travel agencies have recommended. Instead, we have been instrumental in the legal protection of terrestrial and marine habitats here and in various parts of Costa Rica. We have developed a 'win-win' sustainable business in reforestation and eco-tourism.
In our use of architecture, our activities, our dispersal of human density—from the beginning we wanted not to dominate and exploit, but to co-create and prosper symbiotically. Biologically, aesthetically, culturally, morally, spiritually, we have tried not to exceed this place's 'carrying capacity'. We do not want the magic of this place to dissipate.

"We are blessed here with an abundance of really beautiful flora and fauna, people, views, and things; and tasty things. The fish we eat are freshly local caught and not laden with industrial pollutants. We make juice from weird and delicious fruits like maracuya and guanabana. The hearts of palm are eaten the same day that they are cut. The local people still know what wild native foods can be caught or dug up or knocked down.

"My Costa Rican wife and I feel content that La Cusinga offers these treats and prepares them as they should be.

"If indeed we are what we eat and drink, and see, touch, hear, think, and experience—then we have a very nice opportunity at La Cusinga to taste and feel the wild essence of the tropics."

JOHN TRESEMER, OWNER/PROPRIETOR
LA CUSINGA LODGE
FINCA TRES HERMANAS

RECIPES

This cookbook was written for our guests and our many fans and friends who have requested La Cusinga recipes—repeatedly, I might add. Thank you all for enjoying our food enough to want to try to recreate our recipes in your homes and for your friends. It is a certainty that many of these ingredients will not be available except seasonally in many parts of the world, so we encourage you to do what we do: cook seasonally. To our many friends in this part of the world, here is a cookbook that finally uses the ingredients you will find here in Costa Rica. Hopefully you will no longer struggle to substitute unfamiliar ingredients in recipes from the North.

Recipes, well yes, that's what this is all about, but please remember, none of this is written in stone. I don't cook from recipes, I cook from ideas and inspiration. Our trips to the feria and the visits we make to our farmers are the sources of our recipes. It is okay to substitute when it makes sense, and if and when it works there is great rejoicing; when it doesn't we all hope to learn from it. We hope that you will feel free to do the same, and we certainly won't be offended if you do. Look at these recipes as jumping off places.

The only recipes to adhere to are those for pastries and cakes. Baking is chemistry; cakes rise and pie crusts hold together for a reason. Admittedly, desserts are not the strongest part of my kitchen "game", and for that reason I pay close attention to my amounts and measurements. I am not a good enough baker to start making changes.

Please, when you create your wonderful meals for friends and family, try to observe the principals we cook and live by here at La Cusinga. Cook seasonally, locally, organically (whenever possible), and with an eye toward sustainability. Support your local farmers and food artisans; listen to them and let them be your guides. We owe it to ourselves, to each other, and to our communities to support local producers and local products.

Pura Vida
Chef Dave and the kitchen staff at La Cusinga

For descriptions of, and substitutions for, Costa Rican ingredients used in recipes, see pages 71-74.

Roasted Tomato Soup

SOUPS

We began serving a small cup of a chilled soup as an appetizer early on at La Cusinga. We wanted to offer something more than our basic 3-course menu, but didn't want to concoct an ever-changing roster of bocaditos that would clash with the generally unadorned flavors of our food. A cold soup, a pure expression of flavor, was just the thing to cool and greet the hot and travel-weary dinner guest before the larger plates arrived. It opens his or her palate and provides a glimpse of the simplicity and trust in the ingredients that we believe in. There is no dairy in any of these soups; they are simple, rich purées of fresh vegetables.

Roasted Tomato

This basic recipe has become a staple of our kitchen and the core technique of roasting the tomatoes has found its way into a number of other recipes. I adopted this technique when called upon at various times and in other places to extract flavor from unripe tomatoes. The process of roasting vegetables (or fruit, for that matter) at a medium high heat concentrates the sugars, creates caramelization, and increases and intensifies flavors. It's as simple as that.

Preheat oven to 450°F.

12 ripe tomatoes, cored and cut in half
2 large yellow/white onions, peeled and cut into ½" rings
12 whole peeled garlic cloves
½ cup "good" (not extra virgin) olive oil
sea salt and fresh ground pepper

Pour ¼ cup of the olive oil onto a baking or cookie pan (it will need to have raised edges) and tilt the pan to spread it evenly. Place the tomatoes on the pan, cut side down. Put the onion rings in and over the tomato halves; you want them to be tucked down into the tomatoes so as not to burn. Sprinkle the garlic cloves over all and tuck them down in among the tomatoes as well. Pour the other half of the olive oil over all and put the pan into the oven. Roast the tomatoes for 30–40 minutes or until the tops begin to shrink and turn a golden brown color. Remove the tomatoes from the oven and let them cool.

When the tomatoes are cool enough to work with, transfer them to a blender (or you can use an immersion "stick" blender), making sure to get all the liquids and scraping the pan to remove all the stuck-on bits. Add 1 cup of water and purée the soup until smooth. Using a spoon, check for flavor (salt and pepper) and consistency. You may want to wait to add water until the soup "sets". If you have the time, allow the soup (and all our soups) to cool overnight to wait for the flavors to develop. This is your basic tomato soup, to be served hot or cold.

There are a number of flavor options that can used to bump up or change the flavor of this soup, and the flavors I prefer most are acids. Because of the concentration of the sugars in the tomatoes, the original acids have been cooked away and now new and different ones can be added for additional depth.

Because this soup is always served as a cold first course, we like to give it a bit of a bite and to do that add the fresh juice of a couple of mandarinas or limes (add the juice bit by bit, it can creep up). Or, for a more refined taste, add a couple of dashes of sherry vinegar. Another option is to add a favorite style of hot sauce, or combine any of the above flavors.

When there are leftover marinated tomatoes from salad preparations, wait until the next day when the tomatoes have broken down a bit and then purée them and the marinating liquid into the chilled "set" soup. Or, add a quarter to a half cup of extra virgin olive oil to the chilled soup with the blender running, to add a rich suaveness to the soup. The options are plentiful once you have mastered the basic recipe.

Curried Cauliflower

This is quite a simple soup, but the combination of the curry and the cauliflower is a perfect match. When we purée this soup at the restaurant, heads turn as the smell of the curry is so pervasive. The intensity of flavor in this soup is achieved by making sure the curry powder gets cooked.

2 yellow/white onions, diced
2 tbs light cooking oil
2 tbs fresh* curry powder
1 head cauliflower, rough chopped, green parts removed
1 baking potato or 2 medium white boiling potatoes, peeled and cut in large dice
sea salt

Heat the cooking oil and add the onions, curry powder, and salt. Sauté until the onions are bright yellow and appear to have absorbed the curry powder. Add the cauliflower pieces and stir until they are coated and yellow. Add 4 cups of water and set heat to high. Add the diced potato to the liquid. Bring to a boil, then reduce heat to a medium simmer and cook until the potatoes are tender. Let the soup cool until it can be handled without danger and then purée in batches to smooth.

Like all the soups we make, this is best if allowed to sit overnight before correcting the seasoning (salt) and before thinning. It will need to be thinned, as the starch from the potatoes will thicken it naturally overnight. All you will need to do is stir in water until you reach a consistency you like.

- "Fresh" curry powder refers to curry powder that has not been in your pantry for a year or more.

Carrot/Beet/Ginger

This is one of my favorite soups both to make and to eat because the smell of the cooking ginger and the Thai curry paste are rich and deep as they sauté in the oil. As for eating, this soup has such a brightness of flavor that it seems to jump on your palate.

This soup began as a simple and classic carrot-ginger purée and it just kept growing. When we wanted more color, it seemed obvious to use the beautiful organic beets that we keep pickled for salads. For just a hint more complexity of flavor, the Thai curry paste (which we also keep around the restaurant) was perfect as a complementary flavor. And lastly, after making this a few times we decided we wanted to amplify the sweetness just enough to catch the eater's attention, so began using orange juice and then finally, orange-carrot juice for the puréeing liquid.

2 tbs light cooking oil
2 large yellow/white onions, diced
12 carrots, cut into oval rings (oval rings don't roll on the cutting board)
1 knob of fresh ginger (about the size of your thumb, or a bit bigger), peeled and grated
1 tsp Thai curry paste (red or yellow is best, but I also like massaman)
1 large or 2 medium beets, peeled and cut into large dice
1 quart orange-carrot juice (straight oj is a suitable substitute)
sea salt and fresh ground black pepper

Heat the cooking oil in a heavy pot and add the onions, ginger, curry paste, salt and pepper; sauté until the smell is aromatic from the curry paste and the onions are translucent. Add the carrots and stir well to coat. Cover the vegetables with 4 cups of water (just to cover, you don't want them swimming) and bring to a boil. When the liquid has boiled, add the cut beets and return to a boil. Reduce the heat to a medium simmer and cook until the carrots are quite tender and the liquid is just at the level of the vegetables. Remove from heat to cool.

When the soup is cool enough to handle without danger, purée it in batches, using the juice to augment the liquid remaining in the soup pot. If it appears that there is lot of liquid left, don't be afraid to pour a bit off. You want to be able to use enough of the fruit juice to impart some flavor.

Again, we encourage you to let this soup sit overnight for the flavors to "marry". Although it is served and well-loved cold (after all, we are in the tropics), I'm certain it is wonderful served hot on a cold night. Apt accompaniments or garnishes to this soup are sour cream or a natural yogurt. We use a goat's milk yogurt that we buy from the Mennonites at the feria here that is great with this soup. At the restaurant, however, it is served unadorned.

Spinach/Scallion

I have always liked spinach soups and when I was faced with the bushels of wild spinach (*espinaca* local) that grow all over the property at La Cusinga, the soup-making decision was an easy one. There is nothing like putting spinach into a soup to help reduce the volume of the spinach. This soup has a beautiful deep jade green color, but to preserve that color it is important not to cook the spinach too long.

Our first attempts at this soup were thin and lacked body. We had only been using our big green onions (the size of small leeks) to accompany the spinach and in looking for more body and thickness it seemed logical that this could almost be a potato-leek soup (classic vichysoisse) but with huge amounts of spinach puréed into it. The potatoes were added early in the cooking process and voilá (or perhaps, *entonces*, here) the potatoes added the starch and thickness that the soup needed.

2 bunches (4–6) leeks or 12–14 green onions, sliced in thin rings
8 cloves of garlic, chopped
2 oz light cooking oil
1 large baking potato or 2 medium boiling potatoes, peeled and cubed
4 bunches of spinach (about 8 cups, densely packed), at least partially stemmed
sea salt and freshly ground black pepper (this soup will require more salt than you think)

Pour the oil into a large heavy pot and bring to heat. Add the leeks/green onions and garlic and sauté until fragrant. Add salt and pepper and 3 cups of water and bring to a boil. When the water is boiling add the potatoes and cook until tender. When the potatoes are tender, add all the spinach and stir it into the hot liquid. Put a lid on the pot and let it stand for at least 5 minutes. When the soup is cool enough to handle, purée it in batches, tasting for salt. Allow to cool over night and retaste.

This is another soup that would take nicely to a bit of sour cream or yogurt if you feel that you'd like something more. If you decide you want to serve this soup hot rather than cold, just barely bring it to heat and do not boil it. If it boils it will become bitter and the color will fade.

Roasted Summer Vegetable

Honestly, this soup was developed as a way to use up left-over Ratatouille (page 49), the classic Provençal preparation of eggplant, zucchini, peppers, and tomatoes. We discovered somewhat by chance that when puréed and thinned, it made a great soup. Now, rather than sautéing the vegetables, as we would for the Ratatouille, they are roasted in a bit of olive oil to help them develop yet another level of flavor.

We use a salting and pressing technique to remove some of the bitterness from the eggplant that you may not need if you have them fresh from the garden or market. After the eggplant are peeled and cubed, toss them with a tablespoon of salt and place them in a colander with a weighted plate on top. The water in the eggplant (which contains the bitterness developed once the eggplant is off the vine) will drip out and you can squeeze out more after 10 or 15 minutes of pressing.

Preheat oven to 450°F.

1 eggplant, peeled and cut into 1" dice, salted and pressed
2 ayote tierno, cut into 1" dice
2 red bell peppers, cut into 1" dice
1 large yellow/white onion, cut into large dice
3 ripe tomatoes, cored and quartered
12 cloves of garlic, peeled
½ cup good (not extra virgin) olive oil
sea salt and freshly ground black pepper

Toss all the vegetables with the olive oil and salt and pepper and spread them on a rimmed sheet tray. Roast in the preheated oven for 30–40 minutes, stirring every 10 minutes, or until the vegetables are beginning to get crisp browned edges. Remove from the oven and, when cool enough to handle safely, purée in batches using 2 cups of water to make the puréeing easier. Let the soup rest overnight and check for thickness and seasonings.

This soup is great hot or cold. Hot, it is marvelous with pesto swirled into it and cold, it is great with a drizzle of basil or chive oil (bring a ¼ cup olive oil to heat, add chopped herbs, turn off, let cool and purée).

SALADS

Yes, we get beautiful organic salad greens in the tropics. It was surprising to me how well lettuces did down here in Costa Rica when I returned almost two years ago. Just three years ago, organic greens were sparse and tattered things, poorly brought to market and with a disappointing life expectancy. The only other lettuces available were wilty heads of overgrown generic green leaf. Now available in the market are firm heads of nice leafy lettuces like red oak and decent smaller romaine. Additionally, arugula thrives here and recently we have been getting very nice organically grown watercress.

Dinner salads at La Cusinga are composed of these lettuces, as a base, but always contain a number of other components. From the time of my childhood, when my mother would make fabulous green salads packed with other vegetables, I have been a believer in a nicely garnished green salad. Here we pickle and marinate a great many vegetables for inclusion, but also call on staples like ripe tomato (available here nearly year round), organic cherry tomatoes, avocado, cucumber, hearts of palm, and many more.

Basic Dressing

The basic dressing at La Cusinga is an emulsified vinaigrette. That is to say, a slightly thickened dressing that is held together by adding oil into egg and, in this case, Dijon mustard. Each of those acts as a base and when the oil is added to them slowly they will hold it in "suspension" and keep the dressing from separating. This dressing can be made by hand with a strong arm and a good whisk, but it is easier to use either a food processor or a blender.

1 whole egg and 1 egg yolk
1 tbs Dijon mustard
2 oz good red wine vinegar
juice of 2 lemons
6 cloves of garlic, finely chopped
dash of hot sauce
sea salt and freshly ground black pepper
¾ cup good olive oil (not extra virgin)
¾ cup canola or light cooking oil

Put the first 6 ingredients, plus a good pinch each of salt and pepper into the food processor, turn the motor on and blend them well. With the motor running, begin to add the oil, first in a very slow but steady stream, and then bit by bit, more rapidly. As the oil is absorbed into the egg/mustard mixture you will hear the sound of the motor change slightly as your dressing begins to emulsify.

When the oil is completely added and the motor is still running, add 2 ounces of room-temperature water. Remove the top of the processor or blender and taste your dressing. You may want to add more salt, or perhaps a bit more lemon or vinegar depending on how acidic you like your dressing. This will keep, refrigerated, for up to a week. We keep it in a water bottle with a squirt top for easy application and also so it can be shaken from time to time to keep it mixed.

This basic dressing can be altered in a number of ways to reflect whatever flavors you like.

Caesar Dressing

For a classic Caesar dressing, add 6 anchovies, a bit more garlic, more Tabasco and a heavy dash of Lea & Perrins Worcestershire Sauce to the egg/mustard base before adding the oil.

Emulsified Sherry Vinaigrette

For an emulsified sherry vinaigrette, one of my favorites, substitute 3 ounces of good sherry vinegar for the red wine vinegar and lemon juice.

Emulsified Citrus Dressing

For more of a citrus-flavored dressing, omit the red wine vinegar and use 4 or 5 lemons or a combination of lemon and lime. Here at La Cusinga, where we have so many mandarinas, we use them instead of lemons and love the flavor difference.

Passion Fruit (Maracuya) Dressing

The passion fruit is a remarkably acidic yet richly flavorful tropical fruit, and when it is in season, we make this hand-whisked and unemulsified dressing.

Juice of 4 maracuya (To remove the juice, cut the maracuya in half and pour the sacs and seeds into a strainer over a mixing bowl. Press gently but firmly to pass all the liquid through into the bowl.)

¼ cup good olive oil
¼ cup canola or other light cooking oil
sea salt and freshly ground black pepper

When the maracuya juice is ready, put a pinch each of salt and pepper into the bowl and add the 2 oils slowly, while whisking. Alternatively, all the ingredients can be put in a plastic water bottle and shaken vigorously to blend. This dressing is best used fresh the day it is made. This dressing can also be made with mandarina or lemon juice when a lighter, brighter dressing is desired.

SALAD ADDITIONS

At La Cusinga we are firm believers in a salad not being merely lettuce. We are fond of adding any number of fresh and/or marinated vegetables to the salads here, along with cheeses or crostini topped with cheeses or vegetables. We do a lot of marinating and pickling at La Cusinga and these are some of our favorite recipes.

Marinated/Pickled Beets

I must confess that I was a beet hater until well into my mid-thirties. I blame it all on canned "krinkle-cut" beets as well as my loving mother's misguided attempts to occasionally induce boiled beets into the dietary regimen of her children. It wasn't until I learned about roasting beets, as opposed to boiling them, that I became a convert. Roasting (or baking) beets is as simple as baking a potato, and the flavor derived from the oven cooking has helped me to make converts out of numerous beet haters.

Preheat oven to 400°F.
6 beets, green leafy tops trimmed off (and saved for cooking).

Wrap the beets tightly in aluminum foil and bake for 70–90 minutes, depending on the size. Put a towel between you and the beets and give them a squeeze to see if they are ready. If they give a bit, they are done.

Take them out of the oven, remove the foil when they are cool, and put them under running water. The skins will slough right off when you rub them.

Trim a bit off either end and cut them into wedges. Put the cooled wedges into a storage container, sprinkle sea salt and a hefty pinch of freshly ground pepper over them, and cover with balsamic vinegar. Refrigerate the beets and allow them to marinate for a couple of days before serving. They will get better and better with time and will take on a slightly spritzy pickled character soon. The balsamic vinegar can be used over and over again, but it is best not to "marry" different batches of beets.

Roasted Red Peppers

Roasted red peppers are a staple of our kitchen and pantry and we use them alone, atop salads, and also as an ingredient chopped into countless other salads. Roasting and peeling is a simple operation and doing 6 or 7 of them at a time will yield a jar full of them that will keep for weeks in your refrigerator.

Turn a gas burner on to full flame and place 2 or 3 of the peppers around it. Allow them to char and blister completely on one side before turning them. Rotate them fully until they are charred and black all over, then put them into a bowl with a plate tightly over the top. This will steam the charred skins away from the flesh so that they are easy to peel. Repeat with all the peppers. Allow them to come to cool in the bowl, slough off most of the skins into your organic compost and then clean them under running water. Using a paring knife, cut around the top stem, remove it and rinse out the seeds.

Pat the peppers dry and cut them into strips. Put the strips into a jar, sprinkle with sea salt and freshly ground black pepper, and cover with a mixture of 3 parts olive oil and 1 part of your favorite vinegar. Sherry vinegar is wonderful to use for this, and if there is roasted garlic (recipe to follow) oil in the refrigerator, by all means, use that.

Roasted Garlic

It is easy to love the subtle but recognizable flavor of roasted garlic and the cooking oil that it can be preserved in. We use it frequently smeared across crisp crostini as accompaniments to salads and have been known to toss the sweet squishy cloves right in with other salads.

The oil that the cloves are cooked in takes on a deliciously nutty garlic flavor and is great for drizzling over roasted vegetables, adding to the oil for a salad dressing, or for just dipping with crusty bread.

Most standard recipes call for whole heads of garlic to be roasted in the oven to achieve the creamy spreadable texture desired from the cooked cloves, but by carefully watching and monitoring the temperature of the oil, one can achieve the same results in one quarter of the time on the stovetop.

12–24 whole peeled garlic cloves
½ cup good olive oil

Place the garlic cloves in a small sauté or sauce pan and pour in the olive oil. Put the pan on a stovetop burner with the absolute lowest flame you can get. Bring the olive oil to heat and cook the garlic cloves at that low heat for 15–20 minutes until you can pierce them easily with the tip of a knife. Do not allow the oil to reach a boil. If it appears that it will come to a boil, turn off the flame and allow the oil to cool before relighting the flame to its lowest possible point. When the garlic is tender, remove the pan from the heat, allow to cool, and store the cooked cloves and their cooking oil in the refrigerator in a covered jar. This will keep for an indefinite amount of time, but I can never keep it around long enough to find out.

Palmito Salads

Palmito (Hearts of Palm)

Palmito is a vegetable harvested from the bud and the soft center of certain palm trees, among them the coconut, the acai, and the pejibaye, all of which grow here in Costa Rica. Costa Rica is the largest supplier of palmito to the United States and by the time it gets there, does it ever get pricy. Sadly, the harvesting of the heart of the palm kills the tree and we try to only harvest here at La Cusinga when we are clearing area around the property.

The heart of palm resembles a small albino tree when it is brought into my kitchen, reaching nearly 3 feet in length and thickening toward the bottom. The outer part is fibrous and must be cut away, but the core is tender, crunchy, and pleasantly mild. I like it because of its crisp moist texture, because it takes well to a marinade or dressing, and because I don't have to pay $12–14 per pound for it like I did in the US.

Ironically, much of the native Costa Rican palmito is shipped to the US, where it is vacuum cooked in cans, rendering it bland and limp, and sent back to Costa Rica where it is served in hotel dining rooms to unsuspecting tourists. I am so grateful to be able to work with the fresh product.

We have constructed and created a number of hearts of palm salads while at La Cusinga, but keep coming back to this one. What follows is the recipe for the palmito salad that has become a house specialty and is a great introduction for people who have never experienced real, fresh hearts of palm.

1 pound fresh palmito, cut into thin rings
10 strips of Roasted Red Peppers (page 16), cut into a small dice
2 green onions, cut across the grain as thinly as possible (I use chives or, when I can get them, garlic chives for this recipe; if using them, use 9–10 whole chives sliced as thinly as is possible)
juice of 2 limes
¼ cup good olive oil
sea salt and freshly ground black pepper

Toss the cut palmito with the lime juice and add the peppers, chives and olive oil. Toss well, season with salt and pepper, and toss again. Let the salad stand for at least 2 or 3 hours and then retaste for salt and pepper. I serve this salad alongside dressed organic lettuces and fresh tomatoes.

Frijoles Tiernos

Frijoles Tiernos

Frijoles tiernos are what is known in the United States as fresh shelling beans. There are several varieties available to us at various times of the year at the feria in Perez Zeladon and we love including them, marinated, in salads. One of the greatest things about them, aside from their rich creamy texture, is that, unlike a dried bean, they cook in 35–40 minutes. When they are to be used in salads they should be cooked a bit differently than when they are intended to be served hot.

1 pound fresh shelling beans
1 large onion, cut in large dice
10 cloves of garlic, peeled
3 bay leaves
3 fresh thyme stalks
2 tbs salt

Combine all the ingredients in a heavy pot, cover with water by 4 inches, and bring to boil. When the liquid has boiled, reduce to a low simmer and cook 35–40 minutes until the beans are tender. It is important to keep the heat low as the beans will burst easily if cooked too rapidly.

While the beans are cooking, combine:
1 heaping tsp Dijon mustard
2 oz sherry (or good quality red) vinegar
pinch of sea salt and a few grinds of black pepper
⅓ cup good olive oil, added slowly in a stream, whisking rapidly

When the beans are cooked, put them in a colander or conical strainer and drain. Run cold water gently over the beans until the cooking liquid is rinsed away. Lay the beans out on a baking tray to cool.

When the beans are cool, combine with the pre-made dressing and mix gently.

To finish the bean salad, I add ½ cup chopped Roasted Tomatoes (page 9), 10–12 strips diced Roasted Red Peppers (page 16–17), and chopped green onion, parsley, cilantro, or other green herb. Check for salt and pepper and allow the salad to stand for 2–3 hours before serving. I serve this as an accompaniment to dressed organic lettuces at La Cusinga and often top the beans with crumbled fresh goat cheese.

Marinated Cucumbers

Marinated Cucumbers

We get great cucumbers both from our gardens at La Cusinga and also from our organic growers. They are always crisp and have a very subtle flavor. When served on salads the flavor can be punched up a bit with some good quality white or sherry vinegar, fresh ground black pepper, and, just before they're served, a couple of dashes of sea salt. If they are salted too early before serving they will lose every bit of snap and crispness. These are delicious either tossed or topped with some tangy goat cheese, almost replicating the flavors of a Greek-style salad. We discovered one day, when we were out of white vinegar, that the marinating vinegar from a jar of capers gives the cucumbers an interesting "different" flavor, just as the vinegar from a jar of pepperoncini will contribute a bit of heat.

4 fresh cucumbers, peeled and cut in half lengthwise, seeds removed
2 tbs good white wine or sherry vinegar
3–4 twists from a pepper grinder
1 tbs thinly sliced garlic chives, chives or green onions
½ tsp sea salt

Slice the split cucumbers into thin half-moons and toss with the chives and the black pepper. Allow to sit, refrigerated, for at least half an hour. Just before serving, add the vinegar and sea salt and retoss. Drain with your fingers and serve alongside or on top of dressed greens, with or over sliced tomatoes, and definitely with fresh goat cheese or feta.

Cherry Tomatoes/Tomato Marinade

As much as I love the flavor of a perfect fresh tomato, seasoned simply with sea salt and a droplet of great olive oil, there are times when the tomatoes have not or will not reach that point of perfection. I use this recipe at those times.

l do love this recipe best with cherry tomatoes as I find them occasionally a bit tough or acidic at times and this helps in both cases. When I use regular tomatoes for this recipe I cut them either in wedges or slices, lay them out in a Pyrex or flat sided tray, and pour the marinade over the top of them.

2 cups cherry tomatoes (or 6 diced, not chopped, ripe tomatoes), halved
2 tbs sherry, balsamic, or good red wine vinegar
juice of ½ lemon
3 tbs good quality olive oil (if you have a nice extra virgin olive oil, this is a good recipe on which to splurge)
10 leaves fresh basil, cut in chiffonade (thin strips), or 2 tsp freshly snipped chives
2 good pinches sea salt
3–4 grinds from a pepper mill

Toss the cut cherry tomatoes with the olive oil, vinegar, lemon juice, and salt and pepper. Allow to marinate for at least an hour, add the basil (this is best cut just before adding) or chives and serve alongside or over dressed salad greens. If you are using whole tomatoes, assemble the marinade in a bowl and pour over the tomatoes. Add the herb(s) just before serving.

CROSTINI

When we can find good bread in these parts, or if we have the time to bake our own, we serve variations on crostini alongside soups or salads. Crostini means, literally, "little toasts", and they are made by simply slicing a baguette or other slender bread into thin lengths, seasoning, and then toasting. Drizzle the untoasted crostini with a few drops of the oil from your roasted garlic before putting them into the oven for a few minutes to crisp.

All of the above condiments can be chopped and puréed to spread on crostini, and we are particularly fond of the the purées made from the marinated Frijoles Tiernos (page 21) served alongside the chilled Roasted Tomato Soup (page 9), for example, or the Roasted Red Peppers (page 16) puréed, spread on the toasted crostini and served alongside the bright green Spinach/Scallion Soup (page 12).

There are 2 spreads that we make just for crostini because they are a wonderful compliment to the freshness of just-dressed organic greens. One of the spreads is a goat cheese/roasted garlic/green herb spread and the other is a classic pesto.

Goat Cheese/Roasted Garlic/Green Herb Spread

4 oz of crumbly, softened fresh goat cheese
8 cloves roasted garlic plus 1 tbs of the Roasted Garlic oil (page 17)
2 tbs chopped mixed green herbs (chive, garlic chive, tarragon, parsley, basil)
1–2 tbs buttermilk or regular milk

Place the softened goat cheese, the roasted garlic, its oil and the herbs in the food processor and pulse until the cheese is starting to smooth and turn green from the herbs. Check for density and softness (you want it to be spreadable); add 1 tbs of buttermilk and pulse the goat cheese mixture. If it feels soft enough to spread on a crisp crostini scrape it out of the processor, and if not, add another 1 tbs of buttermilk and pulse the machine again.

Jungle Pesto

The word pesto is derived from the Italian word for pestle, as in mortar and pestle, and for generations in Italian kitchens it has been a disgrace to make pesto any other way than toiling over the pestle, pounding the herbs, garlic and oil together by hand. Since there is no Italian Nonna looking over our shoulder, we make pesto in a food processor, and since we have don't have easy access to the classic pine nuts that are used in Italy, we have substituted sliced blanched almonds, which seem to work just as well.

2 cups tightly packed basil leaves
1 tsp chopped garlic
¼ cup sliced blanched almonds
2/3 cup good olive oil
¼–½ cup good parmesan, grated
sea salt and fresh ground pepper

Put the basil, garlic, and almonds in the food processor with some salt and pepper and pulse grind for 30 seconds. With the machine running, pour in half the olive oil in a slow steady stream. Turn off the processor and add the grated cheese. Turn the machine back on and add the rest of the oil in a steady stream. The pesto should be a bit chunky. Taste for salt and pepper. Pack the pesto into a plastic container (or freeze in a zipperlock bag) and press clear wrap tight up against the pesto to prevent discoloration. I do recommend freezing any pesto you do not intend to use immediately as freezing will hold the lovely bright green color.

FISH COOKING

I love fish—beautiful, fresh, firm, bright-eyed, straight out of the Pacific and right off the boat fish! I have a passion for cooking fish and I have a passion for the amazingly fresh fish that we have access to here on the south Pacific coast of this beautiful country.

We here in Costa Rica are not alone, however, in having beautifully fresh fish. Air travel has changed the way the world transports and sells fresh fish and even if you can't get your fish straight off the boat as I do here, you can find excellent fresh fish if you know where to look. I strongly recommend developing a good relationship with one of the fishmongers at a fresh fish market and then relying on his suggestions. Many of these recipes are interchangeable and will work with more than one type of fish. It is far better to use the freshest fish than it is to use the specific fish called for in these or any other recipes.

Here at La Cusinga we have access to a number of lovely white fish: pargo, dorado, corvine, and robalo that, if you cannot find at your market, are easily replaced in these recipes by striped or sea bass, gulf or Pacific red snapper (rockfish), mahi-mahi, halibut, or even swordfish. The recipes calling for tuna are best done only with tuna, but tuna is now available in many, many fish markets, in the US and Europe. As I mentioned earlier, find a fishmonger you trust, or be brave enough to trust your own nose. Ask to smell any fish you might have questions about. Fresh fish should have little or no smell.

Once you have purchased your beautiful fresh fish, treat it kindly before you cook it. Yes, by all means ice your fish, but do not, at anytime, put it in ice or lay it directly on ice! If you want to ice your fish either seal it tightly in a zipperlock bag and immerse it in watery ice, or put tightly sealed bags of ice on top of it. Do not, under any circumstances, let your lovely fresh fish come in contact with water! As soon as water hits the flesh of any seafood, be it fish or shrimp, the flesh begins to decompose and soften. This is an all too common error practiced at seafood markets worldwide, but that doesn't mean you have to repeat it at home.

Searing Tuna

GRILLING FISH

One of the few things that made me sad here at La Cusinga is that we have no grill, gas or charcoal, in our kitchen, as very few things rival the taste of fresh fish cooked simply over a hot fire. If you choose to grill your fish for any of these recipes (and I would hope that you would!), there are a few guidelines to follow.

Make sure your grill is clean and your fire is hot but not flaming. It is easiest to clean your grill while the fire is hot so it can cook away any grease or flavors that might be lingering from your last time at the grill. Place the grill over the hot coals and let it heat up to the point where the grease is dripping from it. Brush the grill vigorously with a wire brush and wipe it clean with an old towel dipped in a bit of oil. Follow that wipe with another wipe from an old but dry towel.

Allow the flames to die beneath your grill while it heats and when the coals are glowing red hot, but not flaming, it is time to put your fish on the grill. Using your oiled towel (but using a clean spot) make another pass over the grill to oil it. Lightly brush your fish filets with olive oil and sprinkle them with sea salt and a few grinds of black pepper.

Place the fish across the grill grates at an angle (to achieve a nice pattern on the fish) and allow to cook on the first side for 3–4 minutes or until you can sense a crust forming. Using a good metal spatula, give the fish a half turn and cook for another 2 minutes. Gently ease the spatula under the fish and, without moving it much, turn it over. The fish will not require as much time on the bottom side and should be ready in just another 2 or 3 minutes. Remove it from the grill, plate it, and top it with one of our delicious sauces.

Roasted Pargo

Roasted Yellowfin Tuna

ROASTING FISH

Because there is no gas or charcoal grill here at La Cusinga, we have devised a method of first searing and then roasting fish that is a good substitute for the flavors of the grill.

Preheat the oven to 450°F. Heat a non-stick and ovenproof sauté pan (or better yet, a cast iron skillet) until it either begins to smoke lightly or water beads off it if you place a few drops on the skillet. Lightly brush the fish filets with a light olive oil and season with a sprinkle of sea salt and a few grinds of black pepper. Place the lightly oiled fish seasoned side down into the skillet and allow to crisp for 2 or 3 minutes. When the fish has crisped and turned a golden brown (you can peek to see), flip it over with a spatula and put the pan and fish into the oven. I have been known, about 3 or 4 minutes into this process, to splash a little white wine, stock, or water into the pan just to make sure the fish stays moist.

Roast the fish filets for 5–6 minutes, pull the pan from the oven, plate the fish and top it with one of our delicious sauces.

COOKING TUNA

I cook tuna only on the grill or in a cast iron skillet, as I prefer my tuna rare. The Yellowfin tuna that we get here in Costa Rica is a very lean fish and the meat dries out very easily if cooked much past medium rare. I recommend using this method for tuna steaks that are an inch thick or more (2 inches is preferable). If you are using thinner steaks, cut the cooking time substantially.

Heat a cast iron skillet until either it smokes or the bottom of it turns gray. Season the tuna steaks with a good amount of sea salt and about ½ tsp (for each steak) coarsely ground black pepper. Press the salt and pepper into the fish. Use a non-stick oil spray to coat the bottom of the cast iron skillet and put the tuna steaks into the skillet. Allow to cook 2–3 minutes without moving and then use tongs to grasp the steaks and turn them over to sear on the other side. After 3 minutes on the down side I prefer to remove the tuna from the pan and eat it gloriously rare with a great spicy sauce, but you may wish to put the whole pan into a 450°F oven for another minute or 2 to allow the tuna to cook to medium rare.

SALSAS/SAUCES

Without exception, every cooked piece of fish at La Cusinga gets topped with a sauce/salsa made separately. We do not make pan-made or butter-based sauces as our feeling is that these are something one can get at a French-style restaurant. Our focus at La Cusinga is on presenting local coastal Costa Rican flavors. We do serve, upon occasion, depending on the fish and the way it is to be cooked, an egg and olive oil based (or aioli-style) sauce.

It is our goal to serve our fresh fish with salsas that are bright not only in color but in flavor as well. So many of the local fruits, particularly when combined with a bit of citrus, lend themselves very nicely to, if not a marriage, at least a lovely relationship with fresh fish. Mango, pineapple, papaya, even our local honey-sweet canteloupe—all these fruits make wonderful vibrant salsas for fresh and freshly cooked fish.

It is important, of course, that you choose fresh fruit for these salsas, but equally important is that the ingredients be cut correctly. When you cut (and please notice I say "cut" and not "chop") the fruit and vegetables, try to cut the pieces as uniformly as is possible. The flavors will blend more evenly and the salsa will have a greater eye appeal.

Additionally, it is vital to the integrity of these salsas that you use your sharpest knife when cutting the fruits and vegetables. A dull knife will crush the ingredients, particularly the onions and peppers, causing them to "bleed" or "weep" out their water, diluting the salsa.

Mango Salsa

This is a basic salsa recipe and can be applied to just about all tropical fruits. As simple as it is however, if the mango is perfectly ripe, this salsa is sublime.

1 fresh ripe mango, peeled and cut in ¼" dice
1 small red onion, diced small and evenly
1 small to medium red bell pepper, cored, seeded, and diced small and evenly
½ jalapeño chile, seeded and minced fine (or a few drops of your favorite "chilero")
juice of 1 mandarina (or 2 small limes)
2 tbs chopped cilantro or culantro coyote
sea salt and freshly ground black pepper

Toss the mango, onion, pepper, and jalapeño together and let stand for at least an hour. Half an hour before serving add the citrus juice, the cilantro, a pinch of sea salt, and a grind of fresh pepper. Retoss the salsa and allow to stand. Serve over grilled fish.

Pineapple-Ginger Salsa

Pineapple is, of course, a staple here in Costa Rica and we have worked hard to incorporate its natural acid sweetness into many of the dishes we serve. This salsa is another that we turn to quite often. When the *pinas* are ripe, there are few better combinations with the sweet white flesh of pargo or corvina. The ginger is a perfect combination with the acid/sweet flavor of the pineapple and when combined with the chile gives the salsa a surprise hit of heat.

½ fresh ripe pineapple, peeled, cored, and cut in ¼" dice
1 red onion, cut evenly in ¼" dice
1 large red bell pepper, cut evenly in ¼" dice
1 jalapeño chile, seeded and minced fine
knob of fresh ginger, about the size of the first digit of your thumb, peeled and finely
    grated
juice of 1 mandarina (or 2 small limes)
3 tbs chopped cilantro or culantro coyote
sea salt and freshly ground black pepper

Toss the pineapple, onion, pepper, chile, and ginger together and allow to stand for at least an hour. Add the citrus juice, cilantro, 2 pinches of sea salt, and a grind or 2 of black pepper; remix and allow to stand for 30 minutes. This salsa will release more liquid when the salt hits the fruit, and the juice is wonderful drizzled over the fish after the salsa is spooned on top of it.

Papaya-Mandarina "Citrus-ette"

We call this brightly flavored papaya sauce a "citrus-ette" (a word we made up) as it is an emulsion of fruit, citrus, and olive oil, much like a salad dressing. We love it over fresh grilled fish with a sprinkle of chopped cilantro, diced chives, or green onions over the top.

½ ripe papaya, peeled and seeded, cut into chunks
1 small red onion, diced
1 small or medium red bell pepper, diced
½ jalapeño, seeded and minced (or a few shakes of your favorite chilero)
juice of 2 mandarinas (or 3 limes)
½ cup good olive oil
sea salt and freshly ground black pepper

Place all ingredients except the olive oil in a blender and purée until well blended but not completely smooth. Turn off the blender. Remove the plastic piece at the top of the blender and put the top back on. With the motor running, pour in the olive oil in a slow steady stream until it is fully incorporated. Check for salt and pepper. Leave this "citrusette" at room temperature if you are planning on serving it soon after making it, or, if you are planning on refrigerating it and using it later (it keeps nicely for 3 or 4 days), you may wish to bring it out to room temperature before serving and may wish to thin it with 1–2 teaspoons of water.

Thai Style Coco-Ginger Sauce

This sauce uses a base of canned coconut milk. When buying it make sure that you don't end up by mistake with the thickened and sweet product made for Piña Coladas. This sauce is made by gently infusing flavors into the coconut milk and letting it stand for a few hours to let the flavors intensify.

1 can coconut milk for cooking
1 knob of ginger (about the size of the first digit of your thumb), peeled and grated
½ tsp Thai red curry paste (use another ½ tsp if you like it hotter)
2 garlic cloves, crushed
½ tsp Thai fish sauce (nuac plam)
1 stalk lemongrass, cut on the bias into several pieces
½ cup cilantro stems, roughly chopped
2 scallions (green onions), cut on a long bias
½ cup cilantro leaves, roughly chopped
juice of 1 mandarina

Pour the coconut milk and bring it slowly up to heat. Add all the other ingredients except for the scallions, cilantro leaves, and mandarina juice, and bring the coconut milk just to a boil. As soon as it reaches a slow boil, reduce the heat as low as you can and allow the sauce to simmer for another 15 minutes, stirring frequently. Turn off the heat and allow the pot to stand, covered for 2–3 hours.

Before serving, pass the sauce through a mesh strainer, pressing to push as much of the solids through as you can. Return the strained sauce to the pan and bring it back up to heat slowly. When it is heated through, add the bias-cut scallions, the cilantro leaves, and the squeeze of lime. Spoon over roasted fish.

Green Gazpacho Salsa

This salsa is adapted from, yes, a Gazpacho soup recipe, and the result is an extremely refreshing and fresh tasting salsa. Remove this salsa from the refrigerator 5 to 10 minutes before serving it over the fish so that it stays cool. The contrast of warm fish and cool salsa is perfect. When you process the cucumbers and other vegetables, try to do it quickly so that there is still some crunch and texture to the salsa.

2 English cucumbers, peeled, seeded, and rough chopped
4 green onions, rough chopped, both whites and greens
1 medium red bell pepper (if you can find one that is in the process of changing color from green to red, use it), cored, seeded and rough chopped
½ jalapeño chile, seeded, and rough chopped
½ cup chopped cilantro
sea salt and freshly ground black pepper
¼–½ cup good quality white wine vinegar
¼ cup good olive oil (extra virgin works nicely in this recipe)

Place the cucumbers, onion, bell pepper, jalapeño, and cilantro into a food processor and pulse for about 30 seconds until they are nicely blended but not smooth. With the motor running, pour in the vinegar and then the olive oil through the top. Add 2 good pinches of sea salt and 4 or 5 grinds of black pepper; pulse briefly and taste first, for acid and then for salt and pepper. If you like your salsa to have a bit more bite, add another dash or 2 of vinegar and do the same with the salt. This is a salsa that should be tasted again just before serving as the flavors of the vinegar and salt will be absorbed by the cucumbers.

A little trick I use occasionally for this salsa is to substitute the vinegar from a jar of capers or even pepperoncini for part or all of the white wine vinegar. The flavor change is substantial and adds a bit of mystery.

Roasted Tomato/Caper Sauce

This is one of the few fish sauces we serve warm. Heat the tomatoes, but do not re-cook them. This calls for tomatoes roasted as for the Roasted Tomato Soup from page 9.

1 cup roasted tomato/onion/garlic recipe
1 tbs capers, with juice
zest of 1 mandarina (or lemon or lime)
juice of ½ mandarina or of 1 lemon or lime
1 tbs water
sea salt and freshly ground black pepper
10 basil leaves, cut into chiffonade (ribbons)

Rough chop the roasted tomato mixture (making sure to use the oil and juices from the cutting board) and the capers. Put them into a stainless or non-reactive pan along with the citrus zest and juice. Bring the sauce to heat very slowly and do not allow to boil. Check for salt and pepper and add the tablespoon of water if the sauce seems too thick.

Add the basil to the sauce just before serving, or, if you wish, sprinkle it over the sauced fish. I like to serve this fish dish over achiote rice or risotto.

Green Herb Aioli

Aioli is a tradition in the Provence region of France. It is essentially a whole lot of garlic and egg yolks pounded together with a mortar and pestle with just enough olive oil slowly drizzled in to make a thick and quite garlicky mayonnaise. The French then gather around the bowl and dip young fresh garden vegetables into it and drink a whole lot of young red wine.

Much in the same way that pesto has been freely adapted by cooks of another generation, aioli has come to mean any kind of flavored mayonnaise, because frankly, when you put the word mayonnaise on a menu, it just doesn't read as romantically and smacks of something you can get at the grocery store. Modern cooks, myself included, and particularly those in a hurry, choose the food processor over the mortar and pestle. The food processor is substantially faster and makes the mayonnaise making process a breeze.

Mayonnaise is an emulsion, and an emulsion is basically a way of putting together two unlike ingredients, in this case, vinegar (or lemon juice) and oil, so that they hold together as a sauce. Generally a third ingredient is necessary to act as a catalyst so that the two unlike ingredients can successfully become as one. Eggs are often used, along with good mustard, as the third, or "binding ingredient" for the emulsion. This recipe uses a whole handful of fresh herbs, along with the egg, as the base for the emulsion.

1 whole egg and 1 egg yolk
juice of 2 mandarinas or 2 large lemons
6 garlic cloves, peeled and crushed
1 cup mixed chopped green herbs such as green onions, parsley, basil, tarragon, chives, or cilantro
¼ cup good white wine vinegar
2–3 dashes of Tabasco or chilero
1 cup good olive oil (not extra virgin)
1 cup light cooking oil
sea salt and freshly ground black pepper

Combine the egg, the yolk, citrus juice, garlic, green herbs, vinegar, hot sauce, a good pinch of salt, and a few grinds of black pepper in a food processor. Turn on the motor and process the mixture for 30 seconds. With the motor running, slowly add first the cooking oil and then the olive oil, pouring in a slow but steady stream. You should hear the motor of the processor make a slightly different sound when about ¾ of the oil has been added. This means the emulsion has been made. When all the oil is added, stop the processor and taste for acid and salt. You may wish to add a bit more citrus and a bit more salt. If the sauce seems too thick, turn the machine back on and add ¼ cup room temperature water to thin. This sauce can be used immediately, but is best the next day. I like to serve crispy roasted potatoes as a side dish for the fish—this sauce is great on them.

Salsa De La Jungla

I had been toying with the notion of creating an all-purpose sauce, one that would reflect what I saw as the basic flavors of our part of Costa Rica. I wanted it to be spicy, sweet, mysterious, and even addictive. It was important to me that it contain only ingredients I could get by walking out the door of my kitchen. I include this in the "fish sauce" section here because I frequently brush it over fish filets in their last few minutes of cooking, but it is equally good brushed over grilled chicken and is particularly good on fire-tinged pork chops or pork loin.

After a bit of experimentation I decided that mango was the perfect fruit for this sauce, but have made versions of it with pineapple and banana as well. Use it as you would BBQ sauce, brushing it on food from the grill right at the end, add a spoon or two of it to a pan sauce for chicken, or add a spoon of it to fresh salsas for a mysterious "picker-upper". This sauce is the essence of the flavors I am trying to capture at La Cusinga.

3 ripe fleshy mangos
juice of 10 mandarinas, the juiced bodies of 2
1 long finger of fresh ginger, grated
1 habañero (or Panamanian) chile, seeded and chopped fine
1 cup tapa dulce, grated from a whole piece

Combine all ingredients in a heavy bottomed non-reactive sauce pot and gradually bring up to a low boil. Reduce the heat and allow to simmer, stirring often, for about 45 minutes or until the sauce has thickened substantially. Remove from heat and push the sauce through a heavy strainer, making sure to push as many of the solids through as is possible. The sauce will keep, refrigerated and covered, for several weeks (it's good to stir it from time to time) and freezes quite nicely.

SHRIMP

Shrimp is a bit of a delicate subject here in Costa Rica. While we harvest some of the sweetest shrimp on the face of the earth, the methods used have caused an uproar in the ecological community. The vast percentage of the shrimp caught in Costa Rica and targeted for export are caught by massive drag trawlers that pull the shrimp and anything else that gets in their path into their nets.

Among the victims of the massive harvesting of Costa Rica's shrimp are the dwindling numbers of sea turtles. The shrimp trawlers are supposed to be equipped with an "anti-turtle" device that prevents the turtles from being dragged in and destroyed, but, as recently as 2009, the United States placed an embargo on Costa Rican shrimp because over 50% of the trawlers arbitrarily tested were making use of the "anti-turtle" device.

It is for this reason that at La Cusinga we will only buy fresh shrimp from fishermen that we know, those who use the old fashioned "cast net" artisan methods of gathering the shrimp. Typically, the old school fishermen gather the shrimp that we use close in to shore, by the river mouths. The shrimp lay their eggs in the relative calm of the rivers and the microscopic hatched shrimp make their way out into the ocean.

One of the shrimpers we buy from, Santos Castillo, lives south of us between Punta Malo and Coronado and ventures out just past the mangroves for his shrimp. The flavor of these shrimp, harvested from estuary waters, is sweet and delicate. He calls me when he has made a particularly good catch and I drive down and buy them from him fresh off his boat.

It is essential when cooking these delicate sweet shrimp that they not get overcooked and so I often will sear them on one side in a pan, remove them, build the sauce in the pan, and then return the shrimp just long enough to cook them through.

Jungle Shrimp "Chef Dave"

I am taking the liberty of throwing my name on this dish because I have never, ever, seen another shrimp dish like this one. This started off in a pretty traditional way, but once I decided to substitute papaya for tomato, it took on a life of its own.

1 pound medium shrimp, peeled and deveined
1 oz olive oil (not extra virgin)
¾ cup diced ripe papaya
1 knob of fresh ginger (about 2" long), peeled and grated fine
2 green onions, sliced thinly
2 oz dry white wine (Sauvignon Blanc is good here—do not use Chardonnay)
¼ stick unsalted butter, cut into small pieces
juice of 1 large mandarina or 2 lemons
8–10 basil leaves, cut into chiffonade (ribbons)
sea salt and freshly ground black pepper

Season the shrimp well with sea salt and freshly ground black pepper.

Heat the olive oil to hot but not quite smoking in a heavy bottomed sauté pan big enough to hold half the shrimp, and sear the shrimp on one side. Remove the shrimp to a plate and repeat with the second half of the shrimp.

Add the ginger and green onions to the pan and swirl; add the white wine and allow to boil rapidly. Add the papaya and toss to mix. Put the pan on the fire and allow to cook for 1 minute. Add the shrimp back to the pan and toss with the papaya. Allow to boil briefly, add the butter and toss the pan again until the butter is incorporated. Pour in whatever liquid was on the plate the shrimp were on. Turn off the heat when the butter is combined and add the mandarina juice and the basil.

Serve immediately over Yucatán Style Green Rice (page 51), Gingered Risotto (page 37) or plain steamed white rice.

Yucatán Style Shrimp

For this dish you will need to make a batch of Roasted Tomatoes (page 9), substituting red onions for yellow and adding a jalapeño pepper.

Preheat oven to 450°F.
8–10 ripe tomatoes, cored and halved
1 large red onion, peeled, halved and sliced into half moon rings, ½" thick
10 peeled garlic cloves
1–2 fresh jalapeño peppers, stemmed and cut in half and then in quarters
¼ cup olive oil
sea salt and freshly ground black pepper

Pour half the olive oil on a sheet pan (with raised edges) and place the tomatoes on it, cut side down. Tuck the onion slices, garlic cloves, and jalapeño pieces down into the tomatoes, sprinkle with sea salt and a few grinds of black pepper, and pour the remaining olive oil over the top. Roast the tomatoes for 35–40 minutes or until the skins are turning a brownish gold color and even darker is fine. Remove the tomatoes from the oven, allow to cool, and rough chop, saving all liquids.

1 pound medium shrimp, peeled and deveined
1 oz light cooking oil
1 cup roasted tomato mixture with plenty of the roasting liquid
4 oz Corona or comparable lighter beer
juice of 2 mandarinas or 3 limes
½ cup cilantro, rough chopped
sea salt and freshly ground black pepper

Salt and pepper the shrimp well. Heat the oil in a large heavy bottomed sauté pan until it is quite hot, but not smoking. Sear half the shrimp on one side and remove to a plate. Repeat with the other half of the shrimp. Return the pan to the heat and pour in the beer, allowing to boil and scraping the browned shrimp bits from the pan. When the beer is boiling add the tomato mixture and bring up to a low boil. Add the shrimp and cook for

3–4 minutes until just cooked through. Turn off the heat, add the citrus and cilantro, taste for salt, and serve over Yucatán Style Green Rice (page 51).

CHICKEN COOKING

We buy and serve only organic free-range chicken at La Cusinga, bought from only one source, for two reasons. The first is that, sadly, it is difficult to find organic chicken here, and the second is that the chickens we do get are just so good. We buy them from Mauren and Ademar at Finca Coreotos, and when I first met them I went so far as to visit the farm to see what the chickens ate. The chickens were feasting on corn and whatever trimmings and cuttings there were from the garden. The meat is moist and flavorful. It tastes like chicken should.

If you are reading this in the US you will have access to good organic free-range chickens and we urge you to avail yourself of them. The difference in flavor is substantial and anything that can be done to put a dent in the sales of mass-produced chickens is a good thing.

Buy whole chickens and break them down yourself. It isn't at all difficult and the bonus is that you end up with good quality bones from which to make stock. Chicken cooked on the bone has so much more flavor so no matter how you break your chicken down, these recipes will work for you. At La Cusinga we roast the breasts so that they retain their moisture and braise the legs so that they stay juicy but become fork tender.

COOKING CHICKEN BREASTS

To cook bone-in chicken breasts, preheat the oven to 450°F. Sprinkle both sides of the breasts with sea salt and freshly ground black pepper. Put an ovenproof sauté pan on medium high heat and cover the bottom with a thin layer of light cooking oil. When the oil is close to smoking, carefully put the chicken breasts in the pan skin side down and cook for 6–7 minutes until the skin is crisp and golden. Remove the breasts from the pan, pour out the oil, return the chicken to the pan skin side up, and put the pan in the oven. If the chicken breasts have all the bones still attached, roast them for 15–16 minutes. If you have partially boned them allow 10–12 minutes for roasting.

When the chicken comes out of the oven, put it on a plate, and pour whatever liquid is in the pan into a cup. Put the hot pan on a burner and add some chopped garlic, chopped fresh herbs (I like thyme and/or oregano), and a splash of white wine. Allow the wine to boil and reduce and when it is nearly gone add 4–6 ounces of good chicken stock plus the liquid from the cup and bring to a rapid boil. You now have a lovely light sauce for your chicken, or the base for something more. At this point we will often add a big spoonful of the roasted tomato mixture, or a fruit glaze, like our Salsa de la Jungla (page 35), bring it to heat and pour it over the chicken.

Braised Chicken Legs

COOKING CHICKEN LEGS

I am a leg man. Give me a chicken and I immediately begin to scheme on a way to serve the legs—umm, love that thigh. I used to have a girlfriend who would only eat the white meat of the chicken and it drove me crazy so I devised a cooking method that even she liked.

The best way to cook a chicken leg, to my thinking, is to braise it. Yes, crisp the skin, flip it over, splash in some wine and stock, and pop it in the oven for about 45 minutes until it is meltingly tender. I have won over numerous "white meat only" people with this recipe. When served over mashed potatoes, risotto, or a good rice, this is tender and delicious.

Braised Chicken Legs

Preheat oven to 400°F.

4 full chicken legs (thigh and drumstick)
½ cup dry white or red wine
½ cup chicken stock or broth
3 cloves garlic, chopped
1 cup chopped Roasted Tomatoes (page 9)

Salt and pepper the chicken legs, dust them with flour, and crisp them in a bit of cooking oil, skin side down in a sauté pan you can put in the oven. Take them out when the skin is crisp and pour out the oil. Return the pan to the flame and add the garlic. Pour in the wine and allow to reduce by half. Add the chicken stock and bring to a boil. Add the tomatoes and the chicken legs, letting them settle into the liquid. Put the pan in the oven and cook for 45 minutes.

Remove the pan from the oven and remove the legs from the pan. Pour the liquid into something that can be easily skimmed and remove the fat from the top. Before serving, return the chicken and the sauce to the pan and put them back in the oven for 10 minutes.

VEGETABLE COOKING

Another passion of mine is vegetables. I made a vow when I returned to Costa Rica in January of 2009 that I would search out and serve only the freshest and best organic produce I could find, and that I would support local growers. That has been my mission.

The second day I was back in this part of the world, Geinier and I visited the teeming feria in San Isidro. There he introduced me to Mauren Jimenez and Ademar Varelas who run Finca Coreotos, a small organic farm in the mountains above San Isidro. Mauren and Ademar (who have since become my good friends) had turned their entire finca over to organic and were pursuing the path of raising the best organic vegetables they could. Mauren and Ademar are responsible for 75 percent of what we serve at La Cusinga and I could not do what I do without them.

It was through an old acquaintance, Linn Aosjia, whose wedding I had catered some years previous, that I came in contact with Marjorie Cerdes Mora and Bolivar Cortes Gomez, the caretakers of Linn's Diamante Organico. Linn's vision had been to build a finca growing exclusively organics in the lush San Salvador valley east of the coast, and Diamante Organico was the farm that came out of that vision. It is from Marjorie and Bolivar that I get the wide variety of amazing and exotic vegetables that make the plates at La Cusinga so interesting.

As I have matured as a chef and a human being, it has become my philosophy that a chef is only as good as his products and that when one is presented with the best possible ingredients the best thing to do is to try to get out of the way and let the natural flavors do the talking. I cook the beautiful vegetables I get from these two couples as simply and respectfully as I can. I am grateful every day for the bounty that I receive as the fruits of their hard labor.

Many of the vegetables that we cook, and particularly the basics, such as green beans and broccoli (which we use a lot of), are prepared by a simple blanching in salted water followed by a shocking in ice water some time before we serve them. Just before they are to be served, I sauté them with whichever seasonings we have decided go best with that evening's flavors.

Green Bean and Broccoli Sauté

fresh green beans, 5–6 per person
broccoli florets, 2–3 per person
2 cloves garlic, chopped fine
8–10 strips of red bell pepper
1 tbs olive oil
sea salt and freshly ground black pepper

Blanch first the green beans and then the broccoli (the broccoli cooks much more quickly) separately in well salted and vigorously boiling water. Using a long strainer or tongs, lift the blanched vegetables into a bowl of ice water. If the water is boiling rapidly, the beans should take 4–5 minutes and the broccoli only 2–3 minutes. Allow the beans and broccoli to cool and remove them from the water. If you are going to sauté them immediately it is not necessary to drain them well.

Heat the olive oil in a heavy sauté pan, add the garlic and red pepper strips, and cook until the garlic gives off a heady aroma but has not changed color. Add the green beans and broccoli and toss to mix with the garlic and red pepper strips. The water on the vegetables should help steam them to hot and they will be ready in less than a minute. Add sea salt and a few grinds of black pepper (I happen to like these kind of peppery) and serve.

Chinese Long Bean Sauté

I am fortunate enough to get beautiful tender Chinese long beans from Diamante Organico and love how they look on the plate when we knot them just after blanching. They will take half the time to blanch that normal green beans take.

Chinese long beans, 3–4 per person
2 cloves garlic, chopped fine
knob of fresh ginger (the size of one digit of your thumb), peeled and grated fine
1 tsp light cooking oil
1 tsp soy sauce
½ tsp sesame oil
sea salt and freshly ground black pepper

Blanch the long beans in well salted and vigorously boiling water. Cook for only 2 minutes and lift from the water and into a bowl of ice water. When the beans are cool, tie them in a classic knot (or knot them twice if they are really long) and place on a plate.

Heat the cooking oil in a heavy sauté pan and add the garlic and ginger, shaking the pan to keep the ginger from sticking. When they are giving off a heady aroma, add the beans to the pan and shake it again to coat them with the garlic and ginger. Add the soy sauce, but do not boil it. Turn off the heat and add the sesame oil, a small pinch of sea salt, and a few good grinds of black pepper. Serve immediately.

Braised Greens

Another favorite of mine and another marvel from the raised beds at Diamante Organico is greens. These are not greens like one thinks of from the American South, however: tough collards and mustards stewed forever with fatback and vinegar. These greens change weekly and there is a mix of 7, 8, and sometimes 10 different varieties in the bags that Marjorie and Bolivar bring me. My mixes do have collards occasionally, but also 3 kinds of kale, different varieties of mustard, wild spinach, different chois, amaranth, wild onions, and more. I love when my guests eat these and then comment on the different flavors they get in the mix. This cooking method also works wonderfully with fresh chard or spinach, although they will not need to be cooked as long.

mixed greens, at least a packed cup per person
3 cloves garlic, finely chopped
¼ cup olive oil (not extra virgin)
¼ cup water
sea salt and freshly ground pepper

Rinse the greens and set in a colander to drip, but not dry. Heat the olive oil in a large saucepan and add the garlic and cook until it releases its aroma, add salt and pepper and the greens, liquid and all. Stir the greens into the oil and garlic, add the water, bring to a quick boil, cover and remove from heat. Allow the greens to steam for at least 5 minutes without uncovering. Before serving, stir greens again and bring back up to heat. I love the braising liquid mixed with rice but you may wish to drain them well before plating.

Choy

At La Cusinga we get 2 varieties of choy from our growers. Choy is an Asian variety of cabbage and while one variety we get, bok choy, grows into a bit of head, the other, called China choy by my growers, is leggy, with almost no base at the bottom. We prefer to season them as we do the long beans, with ginger, soy and sesame oil, but I cook them to done in one pan, allowing more time for the bok choy. If you are using the bok choy, split it lengthwise into quarters or halves if small.

2 bok choy (cut into quarters) or 8 slender China choy
2 cloves garlic, chopped fine
1 knob ginger (the size of the first digit of your thumb), peeled and grated
1 tsp light cooking oil
1 tsp soy sauce
1 tsp sesame oil
¼ cup water
sea salt and freshly ground black pepper

Heat the oil in a heavy bottomed wide sauté pan and add the ginger and garlic. Heat them until they begin to release their aromas. Swirl the pan and scrape the ginger to keep it from sticking. Lay the choy on top and toss lightly to coat with the garlic and ginger. Add the water to the pan and bring to a boil. Reduce the heat, add the soy sauce and cover and steam for 5–6 minutes until the choy is tender. (The bok choy will take slightly longer). Season with a pinch of salt and a few grinds of black pepper and pour the sesame oil over the choy. Swirl the choy in the liquid again and serve.

AYOTE

Ayote is one of La Cusinga's favorite Costa Rican vegetables to cook and something we love to spring on our gringo diners as something they have not eaten before.

Ayote is in the squash family and while it has the coloration of a zucchini, it has the inner seed structure of a pumpkin. Ayote grow to the size of pumpkins and when they are larger are prized here, cooked with tapa dulce and honey, as a dessert.

What we focus on at the feria are the ayotes tiernos, literally "tender ayotes", the small young ones, between the size of a softball and a small cantelope.

Either cut them half, remove the seeds, and then cut them again in wedges or strips for roasting; or cut them in half, hollow them out, and roast an entire half as the base for a vegetarian entrée. Either way, the flesh is rich and delicious when roasted, reminiscent of an acorn or butternut squash, but without the density or overwhelming sweetness.

Roasted Ayote

Preheat oven to 450°F.

2 ayote tiernos, cut in half, seeded and cut in 8 wedges each
1 tbs olive oil (not extra virgin)
sea salt and freshly ground pepper

Toss the ayote wedges with the oil and salt and pepper and place on one of the cut sides on a non-stick baking tray (or one that you have sprayed with a non-stick oil). Roast for 20 minutes, turn the ayote so that the other cut side is facing down, and cook for another 15 minutes or until tender. These can be reheated, but are best served right out of the oven.

Roasted Stuffed Ayote

Roasted Stuffed Ayote

Preheat oven to 400°F

Cut the ayote in half along the hemisphere, and using a tablespoon, scoop out the seeds. Cut a small piece from either of the uncut ends of the ayote so that they will stand upright. Brush the inside of the ayote with olive oil and sprinkle with salt and pepper. Roast for 40 minutes on a non-stick baking pan or sauté pan until the ayote pierce easily with a knife. Remove from the oven.

1 small yellow onion, diced
2 cloves garlic, chopped
1 small red bell pepper, diced small
2 green onions, sliced thinly
1 tbs light cooking oil
½ cup cooked rice
½ cup cooked Frijoles Tiernos (page 21)
3 ounces cheese (I like goat cheese, but a mild white cheese is fine), cut in small cubes
3 sprigs cilantro, chopped
sea salt and freshly ground black pepper

Heat the oil in a heavy bottomed sauté pan and add the onion, garlic, and bell pepper. Add salt and pepper and sauté until the vegetables are tender; add the green onions and toss with the hot vegetables. Add the rice and beans and heat all the way through. You may wish to add a bit of water to make the heating easier. When the mixture is warmed through, fold in the cheese chunks and the cilantro.

Using a tablespoon, fill the roasted ayote halves with the filling and return to the oven. You may wish to sprinkle some bread crumbs or grated parmesan over the top. Roast 20 minutes, or until the top is browned and the stuffing is hot. Serve over rice with some heated Roasted Tomato Sauce (page 9).

Ratatouille

Ratatouille "Cusinga Style"

Yes, we do make Ratatouille here in the jungle and, surprisingly, the vegetables that make this a specialty of the Provence region of France do remarkably well here in Costa Rica. The eggplant, the squash, and the tomatoes all grow happily and flavorfully here in the tropics. One of the things we do here that may be a bit different is to cook all the vegetables separately (except the tomatoes, which don't get cooked at all) and then mix them together when they've cooled slightly. We prefer to have each of the vegetables in our Ratatouille retain its integrity and flavor while still become part of the entire dish. As with the ingredients in the salsa recipes in this book, the cut vegetables for this Ratatouille should be of equal size for cooking.

1 eggplant, cut into ½" cubes, salted and put in a colander with a weighted plate on top to drain
1 ayote, split and seeded, cut into ½" cubes
2 large yellow or white onions, peeled and cut into ½" dice
2 large red bell peppers, cored, seeded, and cut into ½" dice
8 garlic cloves, peeled and chopped
3 ripe tomatoes, cored and cut into ½" dice
1 cup good olive oil (not extra virgin)
sea salt and freshly ground black pepper
10–12 fresh basil leaves cut into chiffonade (ribbons) just before serving

Have ready 1 or 2 flat sheet pans for cooling the vegetables.

Heat ¼ cup olive oil in a heavy bottomed sauté pan and when the oil is hot add the onions and garlic to it. Sauté until the onions just begin to turn golden, turn out onto the sheet pan, and spread them out to cool. Repeat this step with the red bell peppers and when they have picked up a bit of color from the pan, spread them out next to, but not mixing them with, the onions.

Heat the pan and another ¼ cup of oil and add the ayote cubes to the pan. Allow them to stick to the pan a bit to pick up a nice golden color. These will take slightly longer than the onions and peppers, but keep cooking them, stirring occasionally, until they are still crunchy but colored. Turn them out onto a second sheet pan and spread them to cool.

Heat the final ¼ cup of olive oil to almost smoking and after, squeezing the remaining water from the eggplant with your hands, add them to the pan. Let them sit on the first side until they begin to color and then stir. Cook the eggplant for 5 minutes and then turn out and spread on the sheet pan next to the ayote.

When the vegetables have cooled to room temperature, gently mix them together in a mixing bowl, add the diced tomatoes, and mix again. Taste for salt and pepper (the salted eggplant may have given the whole mix enough salt). Allow your mixed Ratatouille to sit for an hour or so to allow the flavors to marry. Serve the Ratatouille at room temperature and, just before serving, cut the basil leaves and toss with the vegetables. This is particularly good with grilled meats or fish.

STARCH SIDES

RICES/ARROZ

Naturally, this being Costa Rica, a country for whom rice is half of the culinary foundation, we typically include rice as an accompaniment to many of our entrees. The national dish of Costa Rica is "gallo pinto", a lightly fried mix of cooked rice, black beans, savory vegetables, and cilantro. Additionally, rice has that wonderful absorbency that has made it a bed for tasty sauces all over the world.

It is easy, however, to elevate your rice accompaniment above the humble steamed or boiled white rice that does seem to be a side to so many dishes here in Costa Rica. The addition of sautéed vegetables, fresh herbs, and either tomatoes or a rich stock can elevate your rice to something that your guests will comment on even if the sauce is a masterpiece.

At La Cusinga we use a oven baking method of cooking (as opposed to boiling or steaming) that is occasionally referred to as "pilaf". This cooking method involves sautéeing the rice and whichever savory ingredients one has chosen in hot oil until the grains are coated and lightly seared before adding the cooking liquid. This method insures that the grains will separate rather than clumping when cooked and also means nothing sticks to the pot. Additionally, cooking the rice covered in the oven allows the flavors to meld quite nicely.

Achiote Rice

This rice dish uses achiote, a paste made from the annatto seed, a brick-red seed with an intense coloring and a minimal flavor. The plant the annatto seed is grown from is also called achiote. It originated among the Aztecs of Mexico and is widely used in the cooking of the Caribbean and Central America. Achiote is used in food dyes all over the world (it is the dye that gives margarine its yellow color) and is often passed off unscrupulously in risottos and paellas as saffron. We use a mix of vegetables along with the achiote to produce a brilliant yellow rice, studded with the bright red and greens of peppers, scallions, or fresh herbs. This rice is ideal served under roasted or grilled fresh fish topped with one of our fruit salsas.

1 red bell pepper, cut in ¼" dice
1 medium yellow onion, cut in ¼" dice
3 stalks green onion, cut in ¼" slices
2 cloves garlic, finely minced
1 ounce light cooking oil
2 cups rice
1 tsp achiote paste
3 cups water, chicken broth, or vegetable broth
2 tbs butter
1 tbs salt

Preheat oven to 400°F.

Heat the oil in a heavy ovenproof pot and add the diced vegetables and the salt. Add the achiote paste and stir to coat the vegetables. Saute until the vegetables soften slightly and add the rice, stirring well. Cook the rice and vegetables in the oil until the rice is completely coated with both the oil and the achiote, then add the water and bring to a rapid boil. Cook the rice at a boil until the liquid has reduced to the level of the rice. It should still be soupy. Add the butter, cover and cook in the oven for 20–25 minutes. Remove the rice from the oven and allow to sit for 15 minutes, covered. Prior to serving, fluff the rice with two forks or a kitchen spoon.

Yucatán Style Green Rice

This rice dish is derived from a recipe learned in Berkeley at the Fourth St. Grill from Chef Mark Miller, and his version is taken from Diana Kennedy, the doyenne of Mexican regional cooking. In this preparation, the herbs and vegetables are puréed with water and become part of the cooking liquid for the rice, turning it a lovely muted emerald green. This green rice is wonderful served under the Yucatán Style Shrimp recipe (page 37) or any roasted fish/salsa combination.

1 bunch cilantro, rough chopped
1 jalapeño chile, rough chopped
4 green onions, green and white parts, sliced in ½" pieces
20 fresh spinach leaves (these help the rice hold its color)
6–8 large dark outside leaves of romaine or other green lettuce
1 yellow onion, cut in ¼" dice
1 tsb light cooking oil
2 cups rice
3 cups water (divided)
1 tbs butter
1 tsp salt

Preheat oven to 400°F.

Place all the green ingredients in a blender with half the water and purée until smooth. Add the oil to a heavy ovenproof pot, add the onion and salt and sauté until the onion is soft. Add the rice and stir well to coat. Pour in the green purée, stirring well to mix, then add the remaining 1 ½ cups of water. Bring to a boil and add the butter. Cook the rice and liquid until they have reached the same level in the pot. It should appear soupy, but you should be able to see the rice. Cover the pot and cook in the preheated oven for 20 minutes. Remove from the oven and allow to rest, covered, for 20 minutes before serving. Fluff the rice with two forks or a large kitchen spoon and serve.

Jambalaya Rice

Jambalaya is, of course, a spicy and flavorful rice dish from Louisiana, generally incorporating sausage, seafood, chicken, and/or whatever the creative cook has in his refrigerator and pantry. At La Cusinga we use the basic recipe for this spicy rice as a base for braised chicken or sautéed shrimp dishes. The tomatoes serve as part of the cooking liquid and the vegetable mix for the rice is what is referred to as the "Holy Trinity" in Cajun/Creole cooking. We use a locally made smoked sausage when making the rice to give it an underpinning of smoke and heat, but it can be omitted. Be sure to cook the spice mix into the vegetables to bring out more of their flavor.

Preheat oven to 400°F.

Jambalaya Spice Mix

2 tbs paprika (use smoked paprika/Pimenton, if available)
1 tsp black pepper
1 tsp salt
½ tsp dried thyme leaves (not powdered)
½ tsp dried mustard powder
¼ tsp cayenne pepper
Blend these well. This recipe makes more than you will need for the rice and will keep in a baggie or jar.

½ pound spicy smoked sausage, cut in small dice or circles
1 green bell pepper, cut in ½" dice
1 yellow onion, cut in ½" dice
2–3 stalks celery, cut in ½" dice
1 jalapeño chile, diced fine
4 garlic cloves, diced fine
2 green onions, cut in ¼" slices
1 heaping tbs Jambalaya Spice Mix
2 cups Roasted Tomato recipe, (page 9), or substitute a 16 oz can of diced tomato
1 cup water
2 cups rice
1 oz light cooking oil

Heat the cooking oil in an ovenproof skillet and add the sausage to brown lightly. When the sausage has rendered some fat and is taking on color, add all the vegetables except the green onions. Stir the vegetables into the sausage and add the spice mix. Cook all over a medium heat until the vegetables are softened and the spice mix is beginning to stick lightly to the pan. Add the rice and stir to coat. Add the tomatoes and water to the skillet and bring to a boil. When the liquid has reached the level of the rice but is still slightly soupy, cover the rice, and place in the oven for 20 minutes. Remove from the oven when done and let stand for another 15–20 minutes. When the rice is to be served, fluff with two forks and add the green onions.

Gingered Risotto

Risotto is an Italian rice dish, generally using Arborio rice. The cooking technique for risotto, adding just a bit of boiling stock or water at a time as the previous liquid cooks in, takes advantage of the starchy nature of this stubby grain and allows it to release more and more of its starch, giving the risotto a natural thickness.

Risottos are often used in place of pasta as a bed for a rich and saucy dish as their very nature lends a bit of absorbency to them. We use a lot of ginger in our risotto at La Cusinga, a decidedly non-traditional addition that lends the rice more of a tropical flavor and incorporates well with either our pineapple salsa or papaya "citrus-ette".

Cooking risotto is a bit more of an arduous task than cooking normal rice and will require your presence at the pot for most of the time, but the rewards in texture and flavor are huge. Be sure to bring your cooking liquid to a full boil before adding it (particularly for the first addition), as this brings out even more of the starch quality of the Arborio rice. Also, it is important to make sure that the rice is nicely coated with oil and vegetables before you add the first ladle of boiling liquid.

6 cups boiling water (or half water and chicken or vegetable stock)
1 yellow onion, cut in ¼" dice
1 knob fresh ginger, about 2 inches, peeled and grated
3 green onions, sliced in ¼" rounds
1 tbs light cooking oil
1 cup Arborio (or other Italian short grain risotto rice)
1 tsp salt

When the cooking liquid has reached a boil, heat the oil in a heavy bottomed pot and add the yellow onion and the ginger. Sauté the vegetables and stir until you can smell the ginger releasing its flavor. Add then salt and then the rice and stir well to coat the rice. Allow it to stick lightly to the pan and keep stirring to scrape it off. Carefully, and using a ladle, add 1 cup of boiling liquid to the rice, stirring constantly. Lower the heat to medium and cook, stirring often, until the liquid has reached the level of the rice. Add another 4–6 ounces of liquid and continue stirring and cooking. As each ladle of liquid is absorbed by the rice, add another and then another. In about 18 minutes, the rice should be ready. Add the final ladle of liquid and the green onions and remove from the heat.

At this point, for the restaurant, we spread the risotto out on a sheet pan to cool so that can be reheated when our guests arrive. If you wish to serve it immediately, allow the last addition of liquid to cook in a bit, but allow the risotto to remain just slightly soupy.

This is delicious, as mentioned, with grilled fish and a fruit salsa, but is also a perfect but different base for a vegetable or shrimp stir fry.

POTATOES

Generally we don't serve a lot of potatoes at La Cusinga. Our cuisine seems to lend itself more to rice as a starch accompaniment, but there are a few notable exceptions. First, when they are available at the feria, we love to serve tiny creamer potatoes that we call "papacitas". These are tiny, not a lot bigger than a large marble, and we either roast them whole or halved, tossed in olive oil, sea salt, and freshly ground black pepper. When they come out of a hot oven in less than 20 minutes, they are golden and crisp and are great alongside a crisply roasted fish filet. This is one of those instances when no other sauce but a Green Herb Aioli (page 34) will do.

There are also 2 purée s that we serve that have become signature side dishes for us. One is a mashed potato recipe and the other uses camotes, the local white yam, and plantains. Each of these is a striking and notable accompaniment to dishes with a great sauce.

Green Herb Mashed Potatoes

For the butter:

½ pound softened butter
20 fresh basil leaves, chopped
4 green onions, green parts only, sliced thinly down to the whites
2 tbs Italian parsley, chopped

Place all ingredients in a food processor and process until you have a fairly smooth green flecked butter.

6 medium white potatoes, peeled and diced large
1 tbs salt
3/4 cup milk
sea salt to taste

Cover potatoes with water and salt and bring to boil. Reduce heat to medium and cook until they are soft enough to pierce with a fork. Drain the potatoes, leaving about ¼ cup of water in the pan. Place the potatoes back over a very low flame. Add the butter and, using a hand masher, mash it into the potatoes. When the butter is fully incorporated and melting through the potatoes, add the milk slowly, mashing as it blends in. When all the milk is blended in, taste for salt. This mash will hold in a double boiler for several hours, but is best served soon after making.

Camote-Plantain Purée

This has become a signature dish of ours at La Cusinga and it is fun for us to watch guests eat it for the first time, look up and ask, "What Is That?" The approach to this is almost exactly like old fashioned mashed potatoes, but with tropical ingredients. We typically serve this purée under a piece of roasted fresh fish topped with Mango Salsa (page 30). There is something about the combination of the mango with the purée that elevates both to a new level. Occasionally, if the mood strikes us, we will put a teaspoon or 2 of freshly grated ginger into the cooking water for more flavor.

4 large white yams, peeled and cut into cubes
1 semi-ripe to ripe plantain, peeled and cut into ½" discs
1 tbs salt
1 stick of unsalted butter
½ cup milk
¼ cup heavy cream
1 tsp tapa dulce or unprocessed sugar
salt to taste

Cover the yams with water and salt and bring to a boil. Reduce to a low boil and cook until not quite tender. Add the plantain and cook until the plantain and the yams are tender. Drain most, but not quite all, the water from the pan and return to a low flame.

Add the butter and, using a hand masher, incorporate it into the yams and plantains. When the butter is mixed in, add the sugar and then the milk and cream slowly, while mashing. When the purée is smooth and all the ingredients are incorporated check for salt and add to taste.

This purée will hold in a double boiler quite nicely, but is best served just after making.

Frijoles Tiernos (Hot)

I must confess to being a bean lover and nothing is better, to me, than cooking a bean fresh from the pod that would normally, to a gringo way of thinking, be dried. In the States, these are called "shelling beans", or, in some cases, "field peas". We buy them at the feria in San Isidro, and during the season, there may be 4 or 5 types available at once.

The immediate joy of these beans is that they cook in 45 minutes or less, cutting at least 2 hours out of the time on the stove. The real joy to them is, though, the flavor and texture. These fresh beans have a richness, a creaminess, and almost a "meatiness" when cooked that is unsurpassed.

When we see them at the feria, they are usually laid out in bins, with a few kilos bagged up ready for sale. It is immediately clear that these beans are different from the ones we typically see dried. They are plumper and more colorful than their dried counterparts and there is a sheen to them, as if they have a healthy glow. The colors range from a pale pink to a mottled variegated pink and white to faint shades of green and yellow. Among my favorites are the heirloom variety, "Cua", which is a yellow-brown color, a bit more rounded than elongated and possessing a deep almost nutty flavor.

We cook these beans much like you would cook dried beans (except for a substantially smaller amount of time), and I find that it's best to start with a sauté of whichever vegetables you choose and the fat and meat from whatever pork product you like to flavor them. Sautéeing the vegetables gives them a greater depth of flavor than just adding them and letting them boil. For additional flavor I like to add a couple of spoons of our Roasted Tomato recipe (page 9), or a handful of roasted pepper strips. You can of course cook these beans in a purely vegetarian style, but they don't call it "Pork and Beans" for nothing.

1 large yellow onion, cut in ½" dice
6 cloves of garlic, minced
1 carrot, cut in ¼" dice
1 jalapeño chile (optional), cut in fine dice
6 strips of bacon, or 1 smoked sausage (hot or mild), cut in cubes; or, 2–3 smoked pork chops (it is quite tempting to use a combination of the 3)
1 oz light cooking oil
1 heaping tbs of "Jambalaya Spice Mix" (page 52)
3 fresh thyme sprigs (or ½ tsp dried thyme leaves)
4 bay leaves

Add the oil and pork products to a heavy pot and bring up to a good heat. If you are using bacon, try to get some color on it. Stir frequently and add the vegetables and the spice mix. Stir often, scraping up the spice mix if it should stick to the bottom of the pot.

Add the beans and herbs (and tomatoes and/or peppers, if you like) and cover by 2 inches with water. Bring the pot of beans to a boil and then reduce the heat until the liquid is just bubbling. Allow to cook for 15 minutes and then check the level of the liquid. It is best if it remains about an inch above the beans. Try not to let the beans cook at too high a heat or they will break up. It is important to keep the beans in enough liquid while they cook, but after about 30 minutes, as they get closer to being done, let the liquid cook down until it is just even with the beans. The beans are done when you can just squish them between your fingers. Remember that they will keep cooking as they cool.

Frijoles Tiernos are great served alongside grilled fish or meat, sausages, or along with either our achiote or verde rices (pages 50–51) for an upscale version of "gallo pinto".

DESSERTS

Our approach to desserts at La Cusinga is that they should be a festive affair. It is our belief that any baked good, be it cake, tart, or torte, is best accompanied by ice cream. We have included the baked items here and the ice cream recipes follow. These are relatively simple cake recipes that I have adapted to suit our needs. Desserts have never been my strong point, so it is important that I keep our recipes simple and follow them exactly. As stated in the beginning of this book, cooking can allow for creativity and can accept a bit of change, but baking is an exact science.

Flourless (Almost) Chocolate Cake with Vanilla Bean and Organic Cacao Ice Cream

Flourless (Almost) Chocolate Cake

This very simple 5-ingredient cake is a favorite with our managers at La Cusinga and pieces left from a dinner in which we had fewer guests than plates of dessert are eyed covetously. Other than following the instructions exactly, the most important step in giving this cake the proper texture is making sure the technique of "folding" is adhered to. Folding in ingredients means to lift and turn them together rather than stirring them in. Folding, when done correctly, produces an airy and lighter cake, while normal stirring causes the cake to be denser and to not rise as much in baking.

When this cake is taken out of the oven it will have risen up to the level of the edge of your cake pan, but when set to cool, it will fall, yielding a densely rich chocolate center.

Preheat oven to 350°F.
200 grams (7 oz) of bittersweet chocolate (we use Torras brand from Costa Rica)
1 stick unsalted butter
¾ cup white sugar
3 level tbs flour
5 eggs, separated

Break the chocolate into pieces and melt it with the butter in a double boiler. While it is melting, separate the eggs and place the whites in the bowl of your mixer and the yolks in a smaller bowl. When both the chocolate and butter have melted, whisk them together and put the bowl on a towel on your cutting board. Making sure the hot bowl is secure, fold in the sugar in 3 additions. When the sugar is incorporated add the 3 tbs of flour and fold them in until just mixed. Turn on your beater and beat the egg whites until they are stiff. Quickly fold the egg yolks into the chocolate mixture and then fold in the whites in 3 batches. Make sure the beaten whites are just mixed in before adding the next batch. This is where the folding technique is most important.

Turn the cake batter out into a pre-sprayed or buttered 10" cake pan and put it immediately into the oven. Bake for 30 minutes and remove to a cooling rack.

The cake will have risen substantially, and now will begin to slowly fall.

Allow the cake to cool fully before slicing. It will cut even more easily if it is refrigerated for an hour or so after it cools to room temperature.

We serve a small but rich and dense slice of this cake topped with either our Vanilla Bean, Organic Cacao, or Caramelized Banana Ice Cream (pages 67–70).

Mandarina Pound Cake with Mountain Blackberry Ice Cream

Mandarina Pound Cake

Pound cake is, of course, an All American recipe, and this one is no different, but it uses fresh mandarinas, the all-purpose citrus for our area of Costa Rica. A mandarina is almost a cross between a lime and an orange, but a bit more toward the lime side as far as flavor. Mandarinas grow all over our property here at La Cusinga and when they are in season they go in just about everything we make. This cake benefits greatly from a good soaking in the syrup made from the mandarina juice cooked with raw cane sugar.

Preheat oven to 350°F.

Dry Ingredients:
1 ½ cups flour
¾ cup light brown sugar (we use tapa dulce)
1 tsp baking powder
pinch of salt
chopped zest of 4 mandarinas

Place all in the bowl of your mixer, turn on mixer, and mix dry ingredients.

Wet Ingredients:
16 tsp unsalted butter, cut in small pieces
3 eggs
4 tbs milk

With the mixer on a low speed, add the butter piece by piece until it is incorporated. It does not have to be creamed. Increase the mixer speed slightly, mix the eggs and milk together in a cup and add to the dry mix. Mix until just blended in; do not overmix.

Scrape the batter into a pre-sprayed or buttered 10" cake pan, place in the oven and bake for 30 minutes. Remove to a cooling rack and pour syrup (recipe below) over the cake as evenly as possible while it is still warm.

Syrup:
juice of 4 mandarinas (⅓ cup)
⅓ cup light brown sugar (we use tapa dulce)

Cook the juice and sugar over low heat until reduced by half.

Allow the cake to sit for at least an hour, but more if possible to allow the syrup to soak into the cake. This pound cake is a perfect match with our Mountain Blackberry Ice Cream (page 68).

"Not Your Mother's" Pineapple Upside Down Cake

This cake has become a signature dessert at La Cusinga and one we serve to large parties and guests who have just arrived in this lovely country. It incorporates 3 signature flavors: fresh pineapple, local organic vanilla, and caramel made from tapa dulce, a raw cane sugar. The caramel flavor that comes from the cane sugar is quite unusual and has a rich earthy quality somewhat like caramelized pumpkin or acorn squash.

The name of this cake refers to a pineapple upside down cake shown on the first page of a Better Homes and Gardens cookbook from the 50s that my mother cooked from extensively. The garish photo showed the cake topped with canned pineapple rings that had been topped with maraschino cherries. This is not that cake.

Preheat oven to 350°F.
Take 3 sticks of unsalted butter out of the refrigerator to soften.

For the caramel:
1 stick unsalted butter
1 cup tapa dulce or other dark raw sugar
½ ripe pineapple, skinned, cored and cut into half moons

Melt 1 stick of butter in a heavy sauté pan and add the tapa dulce. Stir the sugar into the butter very carefully and cook over a medium low heat until the butter and sugar have become one. Continue to cook until the caramel thickens slightly. Pour the caramel into a highsided 10" Pyrex pie pan (I use rectangular for larger groups for easier portioning) and smooth evenly with a rubber spatula. When the caramel is cool lay the pineapple slices in an overlapping pattern around the cake pan, with one end to the center and the other to the outside of the pan.

Wet Ingredients:
2 sticks softened unsalted butter
1 ¾ cups tapa dulce
1 tsp high quality vanilla
5 eggs
¾ cup sour cream or natilla

Dry Ingredients:
1 ¾ cup flour
2 oz ground almonds
1 tsp baking powder
pinch of salt

Mix dry ingredients well.

Cream together the softened butter, the tapa dulce, and the vanilla on a high speed until they become almost whipped. Reduce the speed of the mixer and add the eggs, 1 by 1, and then the sour cream. With the motor running very slowly, add the dry ingredients 2–3 large spoons full at a time, scraping down the sides as you go, until they are all added. Do not overmix.

Gently pour the cake batter over the caramel and pineapple, spreading it evenly.

Put the cake in the oven and bake for 30 minutes at 350°F. Reduce the oven to 300°F and continue cooking until a skewer inserted in the cake comes out cleanly, about another 30–35 minutes.

Remove the cake to a cooling rack and allow to cool for 30 minutes. When the cake is cool, run a knife around the edge between the cake and the pan and carefully invert onto a serving plate or sheet pan.

At La Cusinga we ALWAYS serve this cake with Organic Vanilla Bean Ice Cream (page 67).

Pineapple Upside Down Cake

Basque-Style Almond Torte with Vanilla Bean Ice Cream

Basque-Style Almond Torte

The definition of a torte as opposed to a tart, is that it is baked from a batter that contains mostly nuts and eggs, and that is certainly true of this torte. This recipe yields a cake that is light and absorbent and is a perfect foil for macerated tropical fruits such as papaya or mango (and, of course, a scoop of homemade ice cream).

Preheat oven to 350°F.
8 oz skinless sliced almonds
zest of 3 lemons
1 cup tapa dulce (or other raw dark sugar)
3 whole eggs
4 egg yolks
2 tbs butter
½ cup flour
2 tsp baking powder

Place the almonds, lemon zest, and sugar in a food processor and process until the almonds are finely chopped. With the motor running, add the whole eggs and then the egg yolks through the top of the machine. Drop the butter into the processor and then turn it off. Mix the flour and the baking powder together and sprinkle over the almond/egg mixture. Pulse the food processor just enough to mix in the flour.

Scrape the batter into a pre-sprayed or buttered 10" cake pan and bake for 30 minutes.

Macerated Tropical Fruits
½ papaya, skinned and seeded, cut in ½" cubes
2 tbs tapa dulce
2 tsp honey

Mix the cut papaya, honey, and tapa dulce together in a bowl and let stand, refrigerated, for at least 2 hours. Spoon the fruit and syrup over the almond torte.

Caramelized Banana Tart

Caramelized Banana Tart

For the caramel:
½ cup tapa dulce
½ stick softened unsalted butter
3 large bananas, sliced to ¼" thickness on the long bias

Melt the butter in a heavy sauté pan and very carefully stir in the tapa dulce. Cook until the butter and sugar become as one and then cook until the caramel thickens and is no longer grainy, about 3–4 minutes. Pour the caramel into a 10" Pyrex pie pan, smooth with a rubber spatula. When the caramel has cooled, arrange the sliced bananas in an overlapping spiral pattern.

For the cake:
Preheat oven to 350°F.
1 large ripe banana
¼ stick softened unsalted sugar
1 cup tapa dulce
1 tsp real vanilla
2 eggs
¼ cup sour cream or natilla
1 ¼ cup flour

Cream together the banana, butter, vanilla, and sugar in a mixer until light and slightly whipped. Reduce the speed and add the eggs 1 by 1 and then the sour cream. Remove the mixing bowl from the stand and fold the flour into the wet ingredients, in 3 batches, lifting and turning rather than stirring the flour in. Spread the batter over the caramel and bananas and bake for 45 minutes or until the cake has set.

Remove the tart to a cooling rack and allow to cool for 20 minutes. Run a knife around the edge between the tart and the pan and turn out onto a plate or sheet pan.

At La Cusinga we serve this caramel-y tart with an equally devastating Caramelized Banana Ice Cream (page 70) for a dessert we jokingly call Death By Banana.

ICE CREAM

It seemed natural to us that if we were going to be making different cakes for dessert, that we put a scoop of ice cream on them as well. After all, what's cake without ice cream? So when I came back to La Cusinga in January of 2009, I came back with an ice cream maker jammed tightly into my suitcase. Good ice cream made from high quality organic tropical fruits and flavors was our goal.

Our storage areas are small, so we only keep 5 or 6 flavors of ice cream around at one time, but we have decided which ice creams we think go best with each cake and so while we continue to experiment, we definitely have some favorites. We've focused on using fruit from the La Cusinga property, fruits from the ferias, organic cacao from the mountains near us, and organic vanilla from up the coast in Quepos.

The way we make ice cream is a 2-part process. The first part is making the base, and we do this one of two ways. For most of our fruit ice creams we start with a very intense fruit purée and we build a custard to add into it. We do the same with our organic vanilla bean. The ice creams we make from organic cacao have such a concentration of rich natural cocoa butter and caramelized banana (which is so rich with roasted bananas) that those can stand alone as the base before we add the cream and turn it over to the ice cream maker.

Will you need an ice cream maker to make these desserts? The answer is yes, definitely invest in one. There are number of high quality machines out there for not a lot of money. Even the top of the line machines that we bought for La Cusinga were well under $100.

Vanilla Bean Ice Cream

To make this ice cream, you will first make a custard by adding egg yolks to sweetened milk. It is important that the milk first be added to the yolks off the heat, and quite slowly, to keep the yolks from scrambling.

2 fresh vanilla beans
1 ½ cups milk
1 cup sugar
4 egg yolks
2 ½ cups heavy cream

Put the milk, sugar, and vanilla beans in a non-reactive sauce pan and bring to a simmer. Cook long enough to soften the vanilla beans and melt the sugar. Put the egg yolks into a small mixing bowl and, while stirring, slowly pour a small stream of the warm milk into the eggs. When the eggs and milk have reached the same temperature, pour the mixture into the sauce pan and continue cooking to a temperature of 150°F or when the mixture has stopped foaming and is beginning to settle or thicken a bit. Put the cream in a mixing bowl. Remove the vanilla beans and pass the custard through a fine sieve into the cream. Split the beans and scrape the seeds into the ice cream mixture. Return the beans to the ice cream mixture and allow to cool.

When the custard is cool, remove the vanilla beans and put it into your ice cream maker. Finish the ice cream following the instructions for your ice cream maker. I generally like to let the ice cream go for about 5 minutes longer than the directions call for to get a bit more air into it. When your ice cream is done, spoon it into an airtight container and freeze it overnight to allow it to set.

Mountain Blackberry Ice Cream

At La Cusinga we use local mountain blackberries for this delicious ice cream. The blackberries here in Costa Rica are much smaller than their North American counterparts and seem to be much more intensely flavored. The first time I made this, I wrote to my sister Barbara, who used to be a pastry chef for me, and told her that I had just made one of the five best things I'd ever made in my cooking career. I still feel that way about this recipe.

1 cup milk
1 cup sugar
4 egg yolks
1 ¾ cups blackberry purée (about one and a half pounds of blackberries)
2 ¼ cups heavy cream

For the blackberry purée , place the blackberries into the bowl of a food processor and process until the berries have completely broken down. Pass the purée through a fine metal strainer into a mixing bowl, pressing hard on the solids to get as much fruit and juice through as possible. Use a rubber spatula to scrape the bottom strainer to remove any purée that may have stuck there.

Heat the milk and sugar together in a non-reactive saucepan until the sugar is dissolved. Put the egg yolks into a small bowl and slowly pour a small stream of the warm milk into them, stirring as you pour. When the yolks and milk have reached the same temperature, pour them back into the pan and cook until the custard reaches a temperature of 155° or until the foam begins to separate and the mixture begins to settle or thicken a bit.

Mix the cream and the blackberry purée together in a large bowl and pour the custard into them through a fine sieve. Whisk to just mix the ingredients and chill overnight.

Put the mixture into your ice cream maker and finish, following the instructions. When it is done, put your ice cream into a container and put it in the freezer to set overnight.

Organic Cacao Ice Cream

Here in Costa Rica we are fortunate enough to have access to locally grown cacao beans. The cacao bean is the seed of the fruit often thought of as the culinary nut. These are the beans that cocoa powder is made from, but commercial cocoa powder has had, for reasons of storage and spoilage, the cocoa butter taken out of it. Cocoa is made from the seed powder after the cocoa butter has been removed. The people who grind our cacao beans leave the cocoa butter in the powder, giving it an unusual crunchy texture as well as a haunting and not so "chocolate-y" flavor.

You can make this ice cream with store-bought cocoa powder and it will taste good, but it will not have the same texture or unusual flavor as the ice cream we make here. If you can find organic cocoa powder or the ground beans, by all means use them.

1 cup + 2 tbs organic cacao powder
1 ¼ cup tapa dulce (or other dark unprocessed sugar)
1 ½ cups milk
2 ½ cups heavy cream
1 tsp good quality vanilla

Put the cacao powder and tapa dulce in a food processor and process them until they have blended together to form a rough powder. Add the vanilla to the milk, and with the machine running, add the milk slowly until the powder is blended in (it will not blend in completely). Turn the motor off, add the cream, put the top back on, and pulse the machine 2 or 3 times to blend. Do not run the motor long enough to whip the cream. Remove the ice cream base from the bowl of the processor and refrigerate overnight.

Put the ice cream base into your ice cream maker and finish it, using the instructions for the machine. Put the ice cream in the freezer and allow to set overnight.

Caramelized Banana Ice Cream

It seemed obvious that if we were going to make ice creams that represented the flavors that were all around us here in our rain forest, banana would have to be one of them. It was difficult, however to transfer much of the intensity of flavor to an ice cream, despite the amazing sweetness of our local product. We did a bit of looking around, as well as experimenting, and decided that if we were to cook, that is, to caramelize our bananas, we would get that rich flavor we were looking for. The resulting ice cream has one of the most intense banana flavors you will taste. It is great with anything chocolate and is particularly powerful when served with our Carmelized Banana Tart (page 66).

Preheat oven to 400°F.
10 bananas, peeled and cut into quarters
1 stick unsalted butter
1 cup tapa dulce (or dark unprocessed sugar)
1 ½ cups milk
1 tsp good quality vanilla
2 cups heavy cream

Melt the butter slightly and toss it with the bananas and tapa dulce in a bowl. Transfer the bananas to an ovenproof roasting pan (we use Pyrex) and roast for 45 minutes or until the bananas are quite soft and the caramel formed by the roasting is beginning to stick to the pan. Purée this mixture and allow to cool.

When the banana mixture is cool, whisk in the milk and vanilla, incorporating fully into the mixture. Add the cream without overwhipping and let the mixture set overnight.

Put the mixture into the bowl of your ice cream maker and make the ice cream following the instructions for the machine. When it is done, spoon into an airtight container, put it in the freezer and allow to set overnight.

GLOSSARY OF TERMS/EXPLANATIONS

It stands to reason that there will be a few ingredients here that you may be unfamiliar with, as well as a few cooking terms that I throw around as if everyone had, like me, worked in a kitchen for 40 or so years. Additionally, I will try to add a few explanations for why I do things in a certain way that might not make sense to you. If you have more questions, e-mail me and we'll talk about it.

Tastes of Costa Rica

ACHIOTE

Achiote is a processed paste made from the seeds of the annatto plant. The seeds are a brilliant brick-orange color and are processed with oil and usually garlic. It is sold in tubs in Costa Rica and, as it is also used as a food dye, it will color anything it comes in contact with. Substitution: none.

AIOLI

Aioli is a classic French sauce made by pounding olive oil into egg yolks and a large amount of raw garlic drop by drop. The resulting sauce (an emulsion) resembles a very eggy mayonnaise. The term aioli is used frequently to describe any mayonnaise type sauce because, frankly, it reads better on a menu than mayonnaise does and doesn't frighten diners away.

AYOTE

Ayote is a member of the squash family, much prized in Costa Rica. When young it is known as "ayote tierno", or "tender ayote". Its color and markings are much like that of a zucchini, but its seed structure is more centralized, like that of a pumpkin. The flavor is mild and it is excellent for roasting. Substitution: Young green pumpkins or very, very, very firm fresh zucchini with the seeds scraped out.

BLACK PEPPER

While this is not an unfamiliar ingredient, I cannot stress enough how important it is and what a difference in flavor it makes to grind it fresh. We keep a pepper grinder in the kitchen at La Cusinga and if we are going to be busy we will grind a day's worth in a spice grinder.

CAMOTE

Camote is the all inclusive Tico word for yam and sweet potato, and both grow here. The yams have a purplish-white skin and the flesh is white or a very pale cream color. The sweet potatoes have a reddish skin and the flesh is a brilliant orange. Substitution: White-fleshed sweet potatoes.

CHILERO

Chilero is the generic name for Costa Rican hot sauce. It is generally made with habañero or Panamanian chiles and is blended with a large amount of vinegar, garlic, and salt. It appears, bottled, on the tables at most casual restaurants. Substitution: Any hot sauce that has chiles and vinegar, as its two main components.

CILANTRO/CULANTRO

Cilantro, as we know it in North America, is known as culantro here. It is the same member of the parsley family, has that familiar metallic tang, and is used in salsas and in gallo pinto. Culantro Coyote, while in the same family, a sub-species of coriander, is quite different. The leaves are long, relatively dense, and saw-toothed on the edges The flavors are similar, although Culantro Coyote is stronger, and its flavor holds up longer in cooking and marinades.

FERIA

Feria is a Spanish word which has come to mean a festival or fair, usually in honor of a saint. It is also, however, the Tico word for any open-air market place, generally one that sells produce. It is a farmers market.

FRIJOLES TIERNOS

Frijoles Tiernos are fresh shelling beans. They are commonly sold at the Feria and often are being shelled right there at the table or stand. When cooked they are much creamier and more flavorful than a dried bean and have the advantage of cooking in 35–40 minutes. They come in many colors and varieties, including a common red, a striated pink and white, and my favorite, the "cua", a golden and more rounded legume. Substitution: Any fresh shelling bean.

GALLO PINTO

If there is a national dish of Costa Rica, this is it. It is generally served at breakfast but can accompany all meals. It is a mix of pre-cooked rice, based on a sauté of onion, garlic, red bell pepper and cilantro, and cooked black beans. It is nearly always seasoned with Salsa Lizano, the national sauce of Costa Rica.

MANDARINA

The mandarina is a citrus that grows all over this part of Costa Rica. It is the color of a lime when it is young and its color changes to a pale orange when it is more mature. The flesh is always orange and its flavor is somewhere between that of a lime and an orange, but stronger on the lime side. It is the citrus of choice at La Cusinga and we use it in all recipes that would call for lemon or lime. It is excellent in salsas, on fish, and in desserts. It also makes a wonderful mousse. Substitution: A blend of 2/3 lime juice and 1/3 orange juice.

MANGO

Mangos are native to Costa Rica and I have seen at least 8 different varieties; I'm certain there are more. When they are ripe (when they are soft to the touch—color is not so important) the flesh is aromatic and sweet. We use them in our Salsa de la Jungla (page 35) as well as in a salsa for fish and in a number of desserts and ice creams. A perfectly ripe mango is, to me, the most sensuous of all fruits.

MARACUYA

Maracuya is the Spanish word for passionfruit. The skin of the maracuya here is a pale yellow-green color and is a bit firm. When the fruit is cut open there is a seed sac, protected by a white pith. We scoop out the seed sac and press it against a mesh screen to extract the juice and the pulp. The flavor is at once acidic yet richly sweet. This is another rather sensuous fruit.

NATILLA

Natilla is the Costa Rican sour cream and while it is used interchangeably in recipes with sour cream, its characteristics are a bit different. It responds more like a crème fraiche and is not as thick and dense as sour cream. I use it in place of buttermilk (or mix it with a bit of milk) in some recipes. Classically, in South America, natilla refers to a cooked custard of milk, eggs and sugar, but that is not the case here in Costa Rica. Substitution: Mexican "crema", American sour cream whipped until runny.

PALMITO

Palmito is hearts of palm—the center cut from a variety of palm trees and either cooked or marinated. It is a long tubular tree core and when the outer fibrous layers are cut away, the heart is revealed. The flesh is white and the texture is crunchy and the flavor is mildly sweet. We love to treat it almost as a ceviche, marinating it in the juice of mandarina and olive oil with other vegetables.

PAPAYA

The Costa Rican papaya is a bit different from the ones you may have encountered in other parts of the tropics, particularly in Polynesia. It is larger, not as sweet, and has a decided "funk" to both its taste and smell. There are those who don't like it. I love it and use it in several dessert recipes as well as in a salsa for fish, interchangeable with mango or pineapple.

PLATANO

Platano is plantain, the starchy brother of the banana. It is one of the most common foods in Costa Rica and is eaten fried with the morning meal as well as being served with nearly every casado (a typical plate of a protein, salad, rice, beans and other starches) in the country. I like treating it as the "potato of the tropics", both mashing and frying it.

RICE

I know that we are all aware of what rice is, but it should be pointed out that the rice recipes in this book, with the exception of the Gingered Risotto (page 54), call for a long grain rice. I personally like to cook with a long grain locally grown white rice that comes from the San Isidro Valley, but any regular long grain white rice will do.

TAPA DULCE

Tapa dulce is a raw brown sugar made from the pressings of sugar cane cooked down to a dense syrup. It is generally sold pressed into hard discs in the produce section of grocery stores, but can also be purchased "en polvo", or powdered, in bags. I love the rich, earthy flavor and use it in every recipe that calls for sugar (except those where the color will be drastically altered). To me the flavor is almost like that of the browned edges of a deeply caramelized pumpkin or acorn squash—vegetally sweet. Substitution: Any dense, raw brown sugar.

THAI CURRY PASTE

Thai curry pastes can be bought canned or in plastic containers in the Asian sections of most supermarkets, but one can find a better selection of them in Asian specialty stores. The curries are generally sold in red, yellow, and green flavors as well as massaman. They are made by puréeing hot chiles with a plethora of aromatics, such as cardomom, turmeric, cumin, etc. The flavors are quite intense and I find that a single teaspoon can provide ample heat and flavor to an entire soup or coconut milk based fish sauce.

VANILLA

Please, please, please, do not use artificial vanilla flavorings when making any of these recipes. The flavor of a pure vanilla extract is one of rich and subtle nuances and adds a totally unique flavor to pastries and ice creams. Here in Costa Rica we are fortunate enough to have a rich crop of organic vanilla, and both the extract and seed pods are available.

If you choose to use the seed pods, keep them tightly wrapped and remember to split them before using. When they have been macerated or immersed in a liquid they will soften and the tiny vanilla grains should be scraped into whatever liquid one is flavoring.

COOKING TERMS

There are common cooking terms that I use in this book that I take for granted that my readers will know and understand, but there are also a few that are not so common or at least need to be explained so that we are all getting similar results from these recipes.

BLANCH

Blanching applies to a method of cooking vegetables. When we blanch vegetables we prepare a pot of water, heavily salted and boiling vigorously, and we drop the vegetables into it. They are cooked for a few minutes, to a point of still being slightly crisp, and then they are lifted from the hot water (or poured through a colander) and plunged into an ice bath (this is called shocking). We use this cooking technique for vegetables that we plan to sauté to order just prior to serving.

BRAISE

Braising is the art of cooking in a small amount of liquid—wine, stock, or water—at a low heat. The object is to tenderize, through a long and moist cooking process foods that might otherwise be a bit on the tough side. Generally this is used most with more sinewy pieces of meat such as lamb shanks, chicken or duck legs, or the tougher chunks of meat—brisket, for example. I also use a variation of it on tougher leafy vegetables like collard or mustard greens or kale.

A braise is started by placing the item to be braised in a hot pan with a bit of oil and searing it before adding aromatics, such as herbs and vegetables, and the braising liquid. The liquid is brought to a quick boil and then turned down, and the pan then is placed in a medium heat oven in the case of meats, or covered and put over low heat in the case of greens.

CARAMELIZATION

Caramelization, as it is used in this book, is a method of cooking the natural sugars contained in both protein and produce in order to increase flavor. The reaction of either a meat or a vegetable/fruit product to the application of heat draws the natural sugars to the surface. In the case of meats, searing (or caramelizing, in this case) is a way of sealing natural juices in so the meat remains moist after cooking. When used with fruits and vegetables, it is a way of heightening sweetness and intensifying flavor.

EMULSIFY (EMULSION)

An emulsion is a sauce or dressing that is the result of two unlike liquids (i.e., oil and vinegar) being bound together to create something creamy or thickened. Generally a third ingredient is necessary as an emulsifier to hold the two together. In the case of mayonnaise, for example, egg is the ingredient that holds the oil and vinegar together. Another classic example of an emulsion is Hollandaise sauce, in which egg and melted butter are held together by a combination of cooking the egg and the addition of citrus, which provides acid, a common binder.

OVEN ROASTING

On the surface, this seems like quite a logical concept. Food is put in the oven and it roasts. But the way we apply it at La Cusinga makes it more of a multi-purpose cooking technique. We apply to it vegetables that will be used for soups. We apply it to some of the vegetables that we will serve at dinner (roasted cauliflower is quite delicious), and we use it as a cooking technique for many of our entrée items. We oven roast at 450°F to achieve a level of browning, or caramelization, and when we roast chicken and much of our fish, it is first browned in a pan on the stove top. We use oven roasting as often as we do as the high oven heat tends to help seal in flavor as well as promoting caramelization.

SAUTÉ

Sautéeing is cooking very quickly in a hot pan with a small amount of oil. Generally items to be sautéed are those that will cook quickly. A classic example of a sautéed meat dish would be any kind of scallopini or dish with thinly pounded meat. Shrimp are another example of a protein product that is cooked classically by sautéeing. There are many cases in this book where we call for vegetables such as garlic and onions to be sautéed in order to begin a dish. This is done in order to draw out as much flavor as possible in order for them to contribute to the overall effect of the dish.

SEARING

Searing is creating a crust on a piece of food, nearly always a protein product, by cooking it on all sides over a very high heat. When we sear tuna we finish it very quickly in the oven, and when we sear larger cuts of meat, it is generally to get them browned for braising.

A FEW NOTES AND THOUGHTS ON COOKING

Strong opinions on cooking these recipes and others…

SALT AND PEPPER

You may notice as you peruse this book, or perhaps begin a recipe from it, that I am rather adamant about the salt and pepper that I use. I do not use iodized salt in my cooking unless I am putting it in the boiling water for cooking pasta or blanching vegetables. Period. I don't like its flavor, its distribution is too difficult to control, and it has a tendency to dry out meats, fish, and poultry.

I use kosher salt or finely ground sea salt for day-to-day seasoning and I use larger crystals of sea salt for the final salting of dishes I want to have a burst or "pop" of salt flavor.

I only use pepper that has been freshly ground as the difference in flavor between fresh ground pepper and something that comes pre-ground out of a container from the grocery store (or, God forbid, from deep in the depths of your kitchen cupboard) is such to almost render them different spices. Black pepper was prized by the spice traders of ancient times because of the powerful flavors it releases when it is freshly ground (or, better yet, lightly toasted and freshly ground).

I will generally keep a pepper grinder in the kitchen for quick use, but if I am quite busy, I will use a spice/coffee grinder to grind a quarter cup or so before the start of a shift at the restaurant. Remember that once you start to use your coffee grinder for spices, it is no longer such a good idea to use it for coffee—get two.

OILS

Again, upon perusing this book you may note some ideas on oils, particularly olive oils, that may surprise you. I am a firm believer that olive oil is one of the most overused oils and particularly overused in situations where it has no application. Extra virgin olive oil is a finishing oil! It is NOT a cooking oil. When we do use it at La Cusinga, we drizzle it over sliced tomatoes, over a piece of nice fish that has just come out of the oven, or over toasted crostini.

This being said, I do use a lot of a lighter olive oil for cooking and often I will blend it with a high quality neutrally flavored oil, such as canola, for dressings and sautéeing. I do like the flavor of olive oil, but there are times, for instance, when one is making a salad dressing or aioli, where the oil, if strongly flavored, can overwhelm the flavor of the finished product. When I do the final sauté of vegetables for an entrée at La Cusinga, I will use a small amount of olive oil to perk up the flavor, but when I make salad dressings I use half olive oil and half canola to a) save a bit of money, and b) keep the flavor of the ingredients in the dressing as the ones that "win" in influencing the final taste.

SUGARS

At La Cusinga we are great believers in tapa dulce, a locally produced sweetener made from the extracted and dried juice of local sugar cane. It is often seen as a hard packed disc in the produce sections of grocery stores here, which certainly gives you the notion of something freshly produced. I have discovered a good producer of a powdered variety (en polvo) that I use for most of my baking recipes. I use tapa dulce interchangeably in recipes that call for white sugar with varying degrees of success and as such have noticed that I have had to make a few modifications (which are already done for you here).

It does seem to me that tapa dulce produces a slightly different "sweetness" effect than white sugar does, but I tend to think that my palate has adapted so that I favor it. Caramel, for example, takes on a whole new dimension when made with tapa dulce—one that is deeper and fuller to my taste. Tapa dulce is not far removed from the plants it comes from and as such retains a much more "organic" flavor than processed sugars.

As you have hopefully noticed, there is only one recipe in this book that calls for white sugar, and it's the recipe for vanilla ice cream. The only times I ever use white sugar is when using a darker sugar will drastically alter and/or compromise the color of the finished product.

CREDITS

Cover: Erin Anthony www.silkgrass@gmail.com; dixonindexing
Photos: David L Mahler
Design, Editing, and Indexing: dixonindexing@peak.org
Copyediting: Barbara J Mahler

INDEX

Note: Italicized page numbers indicate photos.

A

Achiote, 71
Achiote Rice, 33, 50–51
Aioli, 30, 34, 71, 77
Aioli, Green Herb, 34–35, 54
Almond Torte, Basque-Style, *63*, 64
Arborio rice, 53
Arroz. *See* Rices/Arroz
Ayote
   about, 45, 71
   Roasted, 45
   Roasted Stuffed, *46*, 47

B

Banana, Ice Cream, Caramelized, 70
Banana Tart, Caramelized, *65*, 66
Basic Dressing, 14–15
Basque-Style Almond Torte, *63*, 64
Beans
   Chinese Long Bean Sauté, 43
   Green Bean and Broccoli Sauté, 43
   shelling, *20*, 21, 55–56, 72
Beet/Carrot/Ginger Soup, 11
Beets, Marinated/Pickled, 16
Black pepper, 71
Blanch, technique, 75
Braise, technique, 41, 44, 74–75
Braised Chicken Legs, *40*, 41
Braised Greens, 44
Broccoli, and Green Bean Sauté, 43

C

Cacao Ice Cream, Organic, *57*, 69
Caesar Dressing, 15
Cakes
   Flourless (Almost) Chocolate Cake, *57*, 58
   Mandarina Pound Cake, *59*, 60
   "Not Your Mother's" Pineapple Upside Down Cake, 61–62, *62*
Camote, 54, 55, 71
Camote-Plantain Purée, 55
Caper/Roasted Tomato Sauce, 33–34
Caramelization, technique, 9, 70, 75
Caramelized Banana Ice Cream, 66, 70

Caramelized Banana Tart, *65*, 66
Carrot/Beet/Ginger Soup, 11
Cauliflower, Curried, Soup, 10
Cherry Tomatoes/Tomato Marinade, 23–24
Chicken, cooking
   about, 39
   breasts, 39
   legs, *40*, 41
Chilero, 71–72
Chinese Long Bean Sauté, 43
Choy, 44–45
Cilantro/Culantro, 72
Coconut milk, 32
Cooking Terms, 74–75
Crostini, 24–25
Cucumbers, Marinated, *22*, 23
Curried Cauliflower Soup, 10

D

Desserts
   about, 57
   Basque-Style Almond Torte, *63*, 64
   Caramelized Banana Ice Cream, 70
   Caramelized Banana Tart, *65*, 66
   Flourless (Almost) Chocolate Cake, *57*, 58
   Mandarina Pound Cake, *59*, 60
   Mountain Blackberry Ice Cream, *59*, 68
   "Not Your Mother's" Pineapple Upside Down Cake, 61–62, *62*
   Organic Cacao Ice Cream, *57*, 69
   Vanilla Bean Ice Cream, 58, 62, *63*, 67–68
Dressing, Basic, 14–15
Dressing, Caesar, 15
Dressing, Emulsified Citrus, 15
Dressing, Emulsified Sherry Vinaigrette, 15
Dressing, Passion Fruit (Maracuya), 15

E

Eggplant, 13, 49
Emulsified Citrus Dressing, 15
Emulsified Sherry Vinaigrette, 15
Emulsify, technique, 14–15, 31–32, 34, 75

F
Feria, 72
Fish
　cooking, 25–26, *26*, *28*, 29
　grilling, 27
　roasting, *28*, 29
Flourless (Almost) Chocolate Cake, *57*, 58
Frijoles Tiernos, *20*, 21, 72
Frijoles Tiernos (Hot), 55–56

G
Gallo Pinto, 50, 56, 72
Garlic, Roasted, 17, 24
Gazpacho, Green, Salsa, 32–33
Gingered Risotto, 37, 53
Glossary, 71–74
Goat Cheese/Roasted Garlic/Green Herb Spread, 24
Green Bean and Broccoli Sauté, 43
Green Gazpacho Salsa, 32–33
Green Herb Aioli, 34–35, 54
Green Herb Mashed Potatoes, 54
Greens, braised, 44

H
Hearts of Palm (Palmito), 6, 14, *18*, 19, 73
"Holy Trinity," 52

I
Ice Cream
　about, 67
　Caramelized Banana, 70
　Mountain Blackberry, *59*, 60, 68
　Organic Cacao, *57*, 69
　Vanilla Bean, 58, 62, 63, *63*, 67–68

J
Jambalaya Rice, 52
Jambalaya Spice Mix, 52, 56
Jungle Pesto, 25
Jungle Shrimp, "Chef Dave," *37*, 38

M
Manarina, 60
Mandarina, 10, 15, 34, 60, 72
Mandarina Pound Cake, *59*, 60
Mandarina-Papaya "Citrus-ette," 31–32, 53
Mango, 32, 72
Mango Salsa, 30, 55

Maracuya, 15, 73
Marinated Cucumbers, *22*, 23
Marinated/Pickled Beets, 11, 16
Mayonnaise, 34, 71
Mountain Blackberry Ice Cream, *59*, 60, 68

N
Natilla, 73
"Not Your Mother's" Pineapple Upside Down Cake, 61–62, *62*
Notes and Thoughts on Cooking, 76-77

O
Oils, about, 76
Organic Cacao Ice Cream, *57*, 69
Organic Vanilla Bean Ice Cream, 58, 62, *63*, 67–38
Oven roasting, technique, 75

P
Palmito (Hearts of Palm), *18*, 19, 73
Papaya, 60, 73
Papaya-Mandarina "Citrus-ette," 31-32, 53
Pargo, roasted, *28*
Passion fruit (Maracuya), 15, 73
Peppers, Roasted, 16–17
Pesto, Jungle, 25
Pineapple Upside Down Cake, "Not Your Mother's," 61–62, *62*
Pineapple-Ginger Salsa, 31, 53
Plantain, 55
Platano, 73
Potatoes
　about, 54
　Camote-Plantain Purée, 55
　Green Herb Mashed Potatoes, 54
　as soup thickener, 12
Pound Cake, Mandarina, *59*, 60
Purée, Camote-Plantain, 55

R
Ratatouille "Cusinga Style," 13, *48*, 49
Rices/Arroz
　about, 50, 73
　Achiote Rice, 50–51
　Arborio, 53
　Gingered Risotto, 33, 53
　Jambalaya Rice, 52
　Yucatán Style Green Rice, 51
Risotto, Gingered, 33, 53

Roasted Ayote, 45
Roasted Garlic, 17, 24
Roasted Garlic/Goat Cheese/Green Herb Spread, 24
Roasted Pargo, *28*
Roasted Red Peppers, 16–17, 21
Roasted Stuffed Ayote, *46*, 47
Roasted Summer Vegetable Soup, 13
Roasted Tomato Soup, *8*, 9–10
Roasted Tomato/Caper Sauce, 33–34
Roasted Tomatoes, 21, 44, 47, 52
Roasted Yellow Fin Tuna, *28*

S

Salads
    about, 14
    Cherry Tomatoes/Tomato Marinade, 23–24
    dressing, 13–14
    Frijoles Tiernos, *20*, 21
    Marinated Cucumbers, *22*, 23
    Marinated/Pickled Beets, 16
    Palmito (Hearts of Palm), *18*, 19, 73
    Roasted Garlic, 17
    Roasted Peppers, 16–17
Salsa de la Jungla, 35, 72
Salsas/Sauces
    about, 30
    Green Gazpacho, 33
    Green Herb Aioli, 34
    Mango, 30, 55
    Papaya-Mandarina "Citrus-ette," 31–32
    Pineapple-Ginger, 31
    Roasted Tomato/Caper, 33–34
    Salsa De La Jungla, 35, 72
    Thai Style Coco-Ginger, 32
Sauces. *See* Salsas/Sauces
Sauté, technique, 75
Searing, technique, 75
Shelling beans, *20*, 21, 55–56, 72
Shrimp
    about, 36
    Jungle Shrimp, Chef Dave, *37*, 38
    Yucatán Style Shrimp, 38–39, 51
Soups
    about, 9, 10
    Carrot/Beet/Ginger, 9, 11
    Curried Cauliflower, 10
    Roasted Summer Vegetable, 13
    Roasted Tomato, *8*, 9–10
    Spinach/Scallion, 12
    thickening, 12
Spice Mix, Jambalaya, 52, 56
Spinach/Scallion Soup, 12
Starch Sides. *See also* Potatoes
    Achiote Rice, 50–51
    Gingered Risotto, 53
    Jambalaya Rice, 52
    Rices/Arroz, about, 50
    Yucatán Style Green Rice, 51
Sugars, about, 77
Sweet potato. *See* Camote

T

Tapa dulce, 45, 61, 73–74, 77
Tart, Caramelized Banana, *65*, 66
Terms, Cooking, 74–75
Thai Curry Paste, 11, 74
Thai Style Coco-Ginger Sauce, 32
Tomatoes
    Cherry, Marinade, 23–24
    Roasted, 21, 44, 47, 52
    Roasted, Caper Sauce, 33–34
    Roasted, Soup, *8*, 9–10
    Roasted Summer Vegetable Soup, 13
Torte, Almond, Basque-Style, *63*, 64
Tuna, cooking, 26, *28*, 29

V

Vanilla, 74
Vanilla Bean, Ice Cream, 58, 62, *63*, 67–68
Vegetables. *See also individual vegetable entries*
    about, 9, 42
    marinated, 16–17, *22*, 23
    roasted, 9–10, 13, 16–17, 24, 45, 46, 47
Vinaigrette, Emulsified Sherry, 15
Vinegar, from jarred vegetables, 23, 33

Y

Yam. *See* Camote
Yucatán Style Green Rice, 37, 51
Yucatán Style Shrimp, 38–39, 51

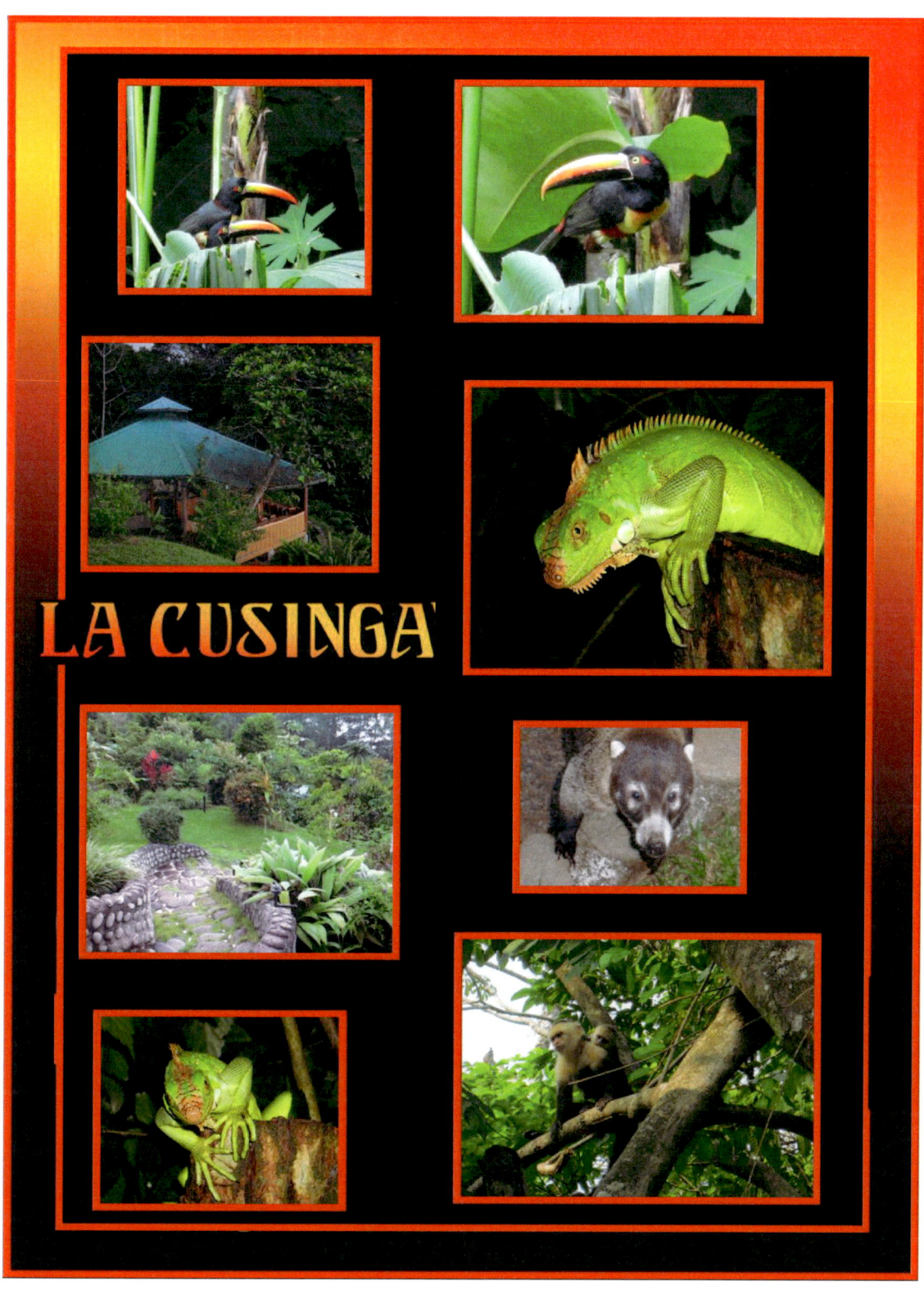

Cooking at La Cusinga, by David L. Mahler